We Had to Get Out
of That Place

We Had to Get Out of That Place

A Memoir of Redemption and Betrayal in Vietnam

STEVEN GRZESIK

McFarland & Company, Inc., Publishers

Jefferson, North Carolina

Library of Congress Cataloguing-in-Publication Data

Names: Grzesik, Steven, 1946– author.
Title: We had to get out of that place : a memoir of redemption and betrayal
    in Vietnam / Steven Grzesik.
Other titles: Memoir of redemption and betrayal in Vietnam
Description: Jefferson : McFarland & Company, Inc., Publishers, 2022. |
    Includes index.
Identifiers: LCCN 2022038292 | ISBN 9781476690513
    (paperback : acid free paper) ∞
    ISBN 9781476648088 (ebook)
Subjects: LCSH: Grzesik, Steven, 1946- | Vietnam War, 1961-1975—
    Personal narratives, American. | United States. Army. Ranger
    Regiment, 75th—Biography. | United States. Army. Aviation
    Company, 174th—Biography. | Vietnam War, 1961-1975—Campaigns. |
    Vietnam War, 1961-1975—Aerial operations, American. | Soldiers—
    United States—Biography. | Soldiers—Drug use—Vietnam. | United States.
    Army—Military life—History—20th century. | BISAC: HISTORY /
    Wars & Conflicts / Vietnam War
Classification: LCC DS559.5 .G79 2022 | DDC 959.7043092 [B]—dc23/
    eng/20220816
LC record available at https://lccn.loc.gov/2022038292

British Library cataloguing data are available

ISBN (print) 978-1-4766-9051-3
ISBN (ebook) 978-1-4766-4808-8

Front cover: The author outside his tent with an M-60 machine gun
(author's collection)

Printed in the United States of America

McFarland & Company, Inc., Publishers
    Box 611, Jefferson, North Carolina 28640
    www.mcfarlandpub.com

Table of Contents

Table of Contents

Preface

"We gotta get out of this place, if it's the last thing we ever do."—Song line by Eric Burdon and the Animals— adopted chorus of the Vietnam soldier

The edicts came in the mail. They stated that we had been selected by our friends and neighbors for the draft, and that under threat of lengthy imprisonment, we were to report for active duty in the military. Felons and college students did not have to go.

Most of us were sent to Vietnam to fight a war that was predestined for failure by the American people and fat cat politicians. Early on I decided I wasn't going to die anonymously and unimportantly. I refused to end as some engraved name; a lost memory of a plodding soldier on some monument honoring the dead. I would ensure my own survival, or extract some semblance of warrior prominence and heroism. I refused to simply be cannon fodder. This book gives glimpses of my journey through the infantry, the engineers, the 75th Rangers, and the 174th Assault Helicopter Company. It has taken me fifty years to write this.

When we returned, we were often shunned.
We were pariahs to some, not heroes.
We were called murderers, but the murderous enemy
was called "freedom fighter."
I was expected to kill my enemy, but forbidden
to berate him by using slurs or epithets.
It was the greatest endeavor of my life;
I couldn't wait to leave there, yet I always go back.
This is dedicated to my brothers-in-arms;
many of whom were braver than I.

1

Introduction
and a Sniper

I was brought up in well-to-do neighborhoods in New York City as the poor kid on the block. My mother, the survivor of a concentration camp, was violent and damaged from her experience. My alcoholic stepfather remained indifferent to me till the day he walked out. A maintenance man and Marine veteran of the Marianas in World War II, he was and remained a drunkard after marrying my mother. The two did little for my self-esteem. Also, possibly a result of my mother's malnutrition while in the camps just before I was born, I was underweight and much too thin well into my teens. For most of my youth, I was easy pickings for bullies because I had the weaknesses all bullies look for. All this made for very poor self-esteem and even less self-confidence in physical altercations.

I finally escaped my parents and the poverty. I moved to Greenwich Village, the epicenter of the hippie and counterculture movement on the East Coast. There, financial status or toughness did not matter. I experienced freedom and unbridled sexuality while developing many new friendships. I lived the life of wine, women, and song for over a year. Then the unthinkable happened. I experimented with LSD and experienced a psychotic reaction, what at the time was called a "bad trip."

The best years of my life turned into the worst in a matter of hours. Overnight I became a shell of the man I'd grown to be. I lost all the newfound self-confidence I'd gained in my year of freedom in Greenwich Village. As much as I'd been happy-go-lucky, I now found myself afraid to make eye contact with people. I had to return to my mother's home, the place I thought I had escaped. There I had to be cared for by her. I endured ongoing paranoia, hallucinations, and her endless recriminations. Then I got my draft notice.

We Had to Get Out of That Place

I resigned myself to my fate. What would be, would be. I didn't care that much anyway because my zest for life was all but gone in my condition. Living in Greenwich Village had been the best year of my life but it felt like a distant memory. The entire counter-culture movement had proved itself mostly theatrical in the long run and had lost much of its luster for me. The Age of Aquarius was not coming. It was a lie. I'd enjoyed wading the waters of the "feel good" mindset but soon realized it had dangerous currents. Free love proved to be less enjoyable love. I tried all the drugs, including the LSD that devastated me. I had no job. It could be said that I was rescued by the Army. I didn't know it then, but the Army would rebuild me into a different person. The nonstop barrage of physical training and interactions with others would snap me back to an almost acceptable degree, and later I would come out on the other end a far different and stronger person than I'd ever been.

To me, those tough guys and hoodlums on the Avenue back home had defined masculinity and toughness till I stood in formation before professional soldiers and drill sergeants. This was a new breed of tough guy. These were different from any men I'd ever met. They had no special hairdos or clothes to give them distinction other than their instructor headgear and the combat ribbons on their chests. They all wore the same green uniform. They never lounged in exaggerated poses. They either stood straight, their bodies in perfect symmetry, or they moved crisply and confidently with long strides. Their faces never expressed any emotion they did not mean to convey. These men were as moving statues. Power exuded from them without any feigned or affected pretense. These were tough men, tougher than any I'd ever met. Their gaze could wither or inspire a young trooper like myself because they seemed so much larger than life. They dwarfed me. I literally and physically looked up to them. I felt we were made of different stuff and I never suspected I would be forged into exactly what they were made of. I was about to be sent overseas and the impact they had on me would change how I defined myself as a man and ultimately, how I viewed the world.

The rigors of basic training hardened and me mentally and physically. All my needs were met and the disciplines of my clockwork routine during this time gave me a sense of security that calmed me. The carefully calculated diet we were fed put weight on me and I developed a lot of muscle that I lost while abusing drugs. By the end of the basic training cycle, I excelled in most of the physical testing and I scored highest in the training company on the horizontal ladder course.

4

1. Introduction and a Sniper

The fact that I did all this in the company of my peers, instilled confidence in me as well. They were all strangers and I was better at this than most of them ... but they were not quite all strangers. There was Gary.

I met Gary in high school. Gary was a big oaf with no social skills and a very low IQ. He operated on such a low level that even the bullies didn't pick on him much. There was no point because he would show little reaction. Big dumb Gary reacted to everything with a big, dumb smile. Gary never knew people were not laughing with him; they were laughing at him. He didn't have a bad bone in his body and for the most part, was a child in a man's body. I felt bad for him because I saw little in his future. He'd remain on the lowest levels of society.

To my great surprise, I saw Gary again in the reporting station at Whitehall Street in Manhattan. He'd gotten drafted as well. His face was as grey as the walls there and his dumb smile was gone. We stayed together on the same planes and buses till basic training at Fort Jackson, North Carolina. He now looked bewildered and afraid all the time. Gary understood his conscripted situation. I doubt he understood the gravity of it. I knew this was a mistake that could not end well. Gary could not run. Gary would be a danger with weapons. Gary could not function under pressure and I knew he would die if he got sent to Vietnam. Our drill sergeants made it clear to us that our survival depended on quickness, alertness, and skill. I doubted Gary understood any of that.

At some point during basic training, the training cadre came to a consensus to "recycle" him. Recycling was a dreaded term for most basic trainees. It meant one had to start basic training all over again. When I heard the news I was happy for Gary. To me, it meant a reprieve for him. I had hoped someone would see that he had no business being in the Army and that the Army had no business with people like him. I hoped he would fail over and over because I knew an eventual discharge was certain. I knew he'd hate it. He'd wonder what was happening to him and there would be tears ... but at least he'd survive.

I never saw Gary again. Years later I searched the list of names on the Wall (Vietnam KIA) and I did not see Gary's. A small sense of relief washed over me.

After a blur of training, buses, paperwork, planes, and holding companies, I received my first overseas orders. I was assigned to the 14th Armored Cavalry Regiment in, Germany. The place was freezing. It was even colder when we had to work outdoors all day on tanks and armored personnel carriers.

We Had to Get Out of That Place

The old-timers' disdain for new personnel was apparent and it took no time at all for me to fall into disfavor with them. The very first night I was scheduled for guard duty on the base runway and instructed on guarding planes. Some of them belonged to high-ranking generals. That night I was tested by the sergeant of the Guard. He appeared on the far end of the runway and I did not know he was the person I saw playing with a plane's propeller. When he did not back away from the plane after my ordering him to, I chambered a bullet and screamed, "Get away from that plane or I'll blow your fucking head off." That episode started my short stint in Germany on a very bad note. Later that week my platoon sergeant ordered me to get new heels on my boots. I made the mistake of telling him they were brand new. When the emergency order for troops for Vietnam came, I was one of the first to be picked. Surprisingly enough, my next unit assignment in Vietnam would have many of the same characteristics, though I would go on to serve in many honorable units later during my time in the Army.

It was January of 1968 and the Viet Cong, backed by the North Vietnamese Army, launched the infamous TET offensive. Battles raged across Vietnam and thousands of U.S. soldiers were killed in a matter of weeks. The casualty rate rose and only started to decline after many weeks of fierce combat. I was a replacement for a dead man but I didn't care. Come what may, after two months, it was a relief to leave the 14th Armored Cavalry Regiment. Twenty-cent bottles of Heineken were the only good memories I carried out of Germany. Thirty days of leave flew by in an instant and when it ended, I reported to an army base in California where we all boarded a jet to Vietnam. The longest flight of my life took me to the longest year of my life.

The day I'd dreaded was coming quickly. I was afraid. I was afraid that when the shooting started, I would be afraid. That thought was more terrifying than anything else. Then, when I actually found myself walking in the jungle on my first combat mission, that thought became unbearable. "Was I man enough?" I wondered as we walked single file. We'd just come out of the jungle and into a rubber plantation. Sun sparkled from the leaves of the rubber trees around me. The heat of the sun creased down between the rows of rubber trees. Time ceased to matter under the weight of the backpack and the tension we all felt. We plodded along. Somewhere ahead of me was the person leading the rest of us. Somewhere ahead of him was a sniper who would try to kill us.

His shots rang out suddenly in three rapid cracks. In a simultaneous dive, we all took cover. I marveled at how different gunshots sounded when they were coming towards me as opposed to when I or my comrades fired our rifles at the range ... a snapping sound by my ear. I was pleasantly astounded that I felt no fear, only a bitter taste in the back of my throat. I looked up and around to see everyone else still hugging the dirt.

The company commander elected to make a sweep to search for the sniper. Where we had been walking single file forward, we simply made a right turn, repositioned, and walked abreast of each other. The tugging sensation of fear welled up in my insides again. Why would a group of people walk directly at a person shooting at them? It seemed suicidal. After a hundred meters I could sense him. There was nothing tangible, just huge spiking jolts of adrenaline as I scanned my surroundings. The feeling was similar to what I'd felt as a child alone and awake at night in a room full of hidden bogeymen. This bogeyman, however, was real. The entire company had walked right under the sniper and I believe I was particularly close when we walked under his tree. I say that because he picked me as his target when he resumed firing at us from the rear. A few bullets struck a tree next to me and oddly enough I felt a strange calm. Then Rosario, the crazy grenadier, ran past me charging towards the sniper. I started to go with him until I was told to sit and take cover behind a tree. I felt sets of eyes on me with the unspoken message that I was asking to get myself killed. We all took cover again.

Whispering our position while crouching low, a radioman called in a gunship. The sniper sat so high up in the tree that the helicopter crew saw him half a mile before they arrived. Now, perhaps beside a tree or maybe still in it, was the crumpled and blood-stained body of an enemy soldier who'd taken a chance and lost.

We sat a while and passed the information down the line about what had happened. Now was a time for reflection. I would find this out many times in the future after firefights. In the subdued conversations they were having, these guys were also letting each other know how they felt. While the sniper never hit any of us, his bullets came perilously close to many of us. It would be fair to say that 15 of us came close to getting shot. We all sat around and talked about it. The smiles and gloating about killing the sniper were a little exaggerated and strained. The original fear felt by us had not gone away, it simply changed into something else. This new feeling was worse than fear, as I would find out time and again. The adrenaline was gone and I was left contemplating the horrendous realities of what had happened. Somewhere back there was a corpse riddled with M60 machine-gun bullets. I wanted to go see him but that was out of the question. In my mind, I laid out as many images of him as I could conjure. Did he fall out of the tree or was he dangling there like some puppet in a horror story? Perhaps he was splayed out on the ground with lifeless, glazed eyes staring stupidly at the sky. Was he bleeding? Christ, the son of a bitch could have killed me. This was insane. Those bullets of his that hit the tree next to me would have torn my body up or killed me if one or two had hit.

I looked at my shoulder and tried to visualize a bullet going through it. I guessed the exit wound would be a mess. The backpack strap would be ruined. *What was I thinking? For God's sake, my shoulder bones would have been splintered. I'd be a cripple for life if I survived.* The change in me was beginning to occur. I started to feel a low-intensity panic that would stay with me. It was not a panic of fright as much as it was a panic caused by the realization of the absurdity and certainty of the situation I was in. I knew then that I would have to keep my wits about me to get out of this alive. I'd instantly developed a survival instinct, a kind of watch-out-for-yourself attitude that I'd never really had before. I also was aware of a growing self-confidence. When the shooting had started I was not the scared little new guy I was so afraid I'd be. On the contrary, I felt I'd handled it better than most. It occurred to me that the reason I'd handled it well was that I was new to it. It didn't matter. I was up and ready when others had been cringing and hugging the dirt. I felt a new assurance and bravado that contrasted the bleakness of my situation. When my platoon Sergeant came to check on me, because I was the new guy, and asked me if I was OK, I looked him straight in the eye and answered, "I'm fine, Sergeant, just fine."

Decades after that first contact with the enemy, I still think of that war. Not a day goes by without my falling into a reflective sullenness. I dwell in it for a while. I think of the guys and the waste my country made of our noble effort. The vain sacrifices made by fallen giants sear me. But war memories are a creeping vine. One must take care to stay untangled.

So immerse yourself in my memories. It is my hope they entertain, excite and inform you. Some of these events may be out of order. I did no research to correct timelines. I write this the way I remember it.

2

In Country

Landing in Hawaii, an island paradise, to get to the jungles of Vietnam struck me as ironic. We weren't allowed to leave the plane lest we wander off and never return. Staring through the oblong window, I wondered what was behind the airport's walls. I imagined tall fruity drinks held by dark-skinned beauties. I pictured them with leis around their necks, greeting people in the Hawaiian tradition. (Oddly enough, on my second tour of Vietnam we went nonstop across Alaska. The curvature of the earth allowed that peculiarity.)

We flew in silence for most of the flight. Our journey had a detached eeriness about it. The stewardesses wore cocked caps, fresh white blouses, and wispy scarves. They served our meals and chatted with us. Possessed of genteel femininity enhanced by simple good looks, they were good-looking young women, serving good-looking young men. But for our khaki uniforms and short haircuts, we could have easily been mistaken for high school athletes going cross country to a championship game. Most of us came from the lower classes. We were young, rugged, and newly strong. Many guys had never worn nice clothes or a uniform before. For them, this was an upscale occasion. The vast majority had hardly finished high school, if at all. Few of us knew the niceties of luxury travel. I considered our destination, and was again struck by the irony.

I would find out later that in the Army, we draftees were considered a lower class. Volunteers were held in higher esteem than draftees. This was borne out in assignments. Draftees got the worst ones. The Vietnam War, for the most part, was fought, and its battles won, by draftees. I compared the grueling four months of extremes we'd endured in training to this comparatively luxurious flight and again saw irony. There was, however, no denying the underlying, ever-present fact that we were flying toward hell. The stewardesses knew it too and were unsuccessful at hiding that knowledge. Their practiced demeanor couldn't mask their tension. It showed in their exaggerated warmth. It was apparent when they looked at us out of the corners of their eyes. You could catch it in their glance if you looked quickly enough.

The flight was uneventful. Some guys napped, some chatted in whispers. When I considered our destination I was struck by the lack of any display of emotion. We stopped in Japan briefly and resumed our flight. The entire flight took seventeen hours. When we started our descent into Cam Ranh Bay, not a sound could be heard other than the diminishing howl of the jet's engines. All eyes looked out the windows of the plane.

We landed. The entrance to hell revealed itself in a burst of sunlight at the front of the plane when the door opened. Though tired, the stewardesses moved faster than they had during the entire time of the flight. As soldiers walked single-file off the plane, the temperature steadily rose inside it. I was halfway back in the aisle and I felt the heat work its way past me. Guys were developing beads of sweat on their necks and faces. Everyone looked uncomfortable. When I got to the front and exited the hatch, a blast of heat jolted me. I turned my head instinctively to avoid the sudden light and heat. The sensation was similar to opening a hot oven door. As my senses adjusted, I realized I was in a pretty place. Through squinted eyes, I saw a vista of palms with green mountains behind them. Turning my head again, I saw the sea in the distance. Below the plane's ramp a "mammasan" in black pajamas and a straw conical hat swept the tarmac we'd landed on. She did so in slow deliberate motions. I might as well have landed for a tropical vacation from the appearance of the place.

I stepped out of the plane onto the old-fashioned ramp; the type that got wheeled up to the plane. Step by step I approached the ground that was Vietnam. Then, as I felt its firmness under my feet, I knew the moment was a milestone in my life. The guy in front of me slowed down and said "Hey, mammasan, how much for a blow job?"

My cheeks flushed. I couldn't believe what I'd heard. His words jarred and disgusted me. "The Ugly American" came to mind. Maybe I'd seen the title on a movie marquee, or on a book in a store. The title was self-explanatory. This ignorant son-of-a-bitch in front of me was the epitome of an ugly American. This woman looked old and noble. She was probably someone's grandmother. I thought of pushing the guy but he was stocky and I already knew he was mean and stupid. I would always remember that incident with great clarity. It was one of the most disheartening moments of two tours in Vietnam.

The hell of Vietnam usually flared up outside the main bases. It played out behind mountains and in fertile fields, valleys, and jungles. The enemy hid in small hamlets and big cities. By day, he often masqueraded as a harmless civilian. Entire, seemingly innocuous, villages could erupt in the gunfire of an ambush. Vietnam was a National Geographic moment gone terribly wrong. Everyone in this country was either trying to stay alive or trying to kill people. In my case, it would be both, and, as I came to find out, how one came home depended on which he was better at. For now, I felt I was in a safe place. Cam Ranh Bay and other major bases did occasionally get attacked. Most of the time, these attacks were by rockets and mortars. Some bases, including Cam Ranh Bay, experienced human attacks. Though deemed a protected area, it actually had the hospital attacked in August of 1969. Bedridden U.S. troops were killed where they lay. The enemy penetrated the barbed wire wearing black. They ran in from the night like some banshees from a horror movie. They sprinted through the hospital throwing explosives. Later, in 1971 they crept through the wire and blew up the ammo dump there.

In most cases, these attacks proved costly to the enemy. Usually, in the morning, many attackers were found dead and hanging bloody in the razor wire of the perimeters. Many were blown to bits or riddled with bullets. I would never experience this type of nightmarish assault in my two tours of Vietnam. I would, however, experience many close calls.

The intake staff at Cam Ranh treated us politely. I noticed a laid-back atmosphere. Sergeants and officers spoke to us as equals. Yelling was only for purposes of projecting voices. These men knew where we'd come from and where we were going. I noticed nobody was saluting officers. This casual attitude was rooted in necessity. Salutes automatically identified officers to the enemy and made them prime targets for snipers.

Names and social security numbers were checked and paperwork was finished quickly. We got assigned bunks in pleasant-looking, clean, bungalow-like buildings. I threw my duffel bag under my assigned bunk and went to the mess hall with a small group of guys to eat. For a war zone, the food was great. When I had some time, I went outside to look around.

We Had to Get Out of That Place

The oppressive heat of the day had given way to a slow, sultry evening breeze. These tropical winds felt and smelled different than anything I'd ever experienced in the states. The heat was no different from many summer nights in New York, yet it had a distinct flavor. It felt foreign and exotic. It carried with it a clean, clear scent. I breathed heavy air laden with a mustiness that hinted some aroma just beyond recognition. The afternoon faded into early evening as I ambled around the area we'd been told to confine ourselves to. I walked by administrative buildings, a post office and random housing buildings.

With the dusk, the sky turned azure, like some big, inverted ocean above me. The horizon brimmed brightly as the sun set. Stars began to poke through the vivid color above me as I shuffled through fine, white sand. My head upturned, I marveled. I had never seen stars this bright in a light sky. I was still standing in my reverie when explosions and gunfire erupted around me.

A sudden blast ripped through the evening air ... then another one. The explosions actually shook the ground I stood on. They started from one direction and spread. Explosions crashed the night air all around me. They sounded like thunder, but much louder. Then, the sound of automatic rifle fire and machine-gun fire surrounded me. The worst-case scenario unfolded in my mind: I was in Vietnam without a weapon during an attack. Worse yet, I didn't know what to do or where to go. Heart pounding, I spun like a madman and looked for cover. All the buildings had sandbags piled three or four feet high around them. I noticed that the sandbags were not actually against the buildings. There was a small clearance between them and the buildings. I immediately threw myself up and over the sandbags of the building closest to me. Then, I wriggled downwards through the tight squeeze. Once I got as low as I could, I found myself staring upward. That would be where the face that came to kill or save me would appear. Within a minute the chaos subsided and then stopped as fast as it had started. I didn't move at first. Then I turned my head. Immediately next to my face lay a rat poison box. I jerked my head back and began the process of wiggling out of there. I still didn't know if I was in any danger but I knew I was semi-stuck in the crevice I'd wedged myself into. With great difficulty, I got myself upright and looked around. No one had seen me. I didn't know whether to run or hide. I straddled the sandbags, jumped off, and stepped away from them in one awkward motion. Then, I started walking away carefully. I felt an overwhelming feeling of embarrassment.

Time crawled. I desperately needed to see an American soldier. Only a few minutes had passed when I saw a sergeant. I jogged up to him and asked him what had happened. He grinned with the slow realization I was a new guy and answered, "That was nuthin' man, just a mad minute."

"Mad minute" is a term coined in Vietnam to denote a period of a sudden, random, break-out of massive firepower. It happened at most bases in the evening. These displays appeared to happen for no reason, but they were rooted in sound logic. They helped keep the perimeters clear of potential sappers or spotters trying to spy on the base. Stale ammunition was used up and later replaced. Soldiers got to practice shooting and relieve some tension. But most of all, everyone catered to the fantasy that they might just kill a bad guy lurking in the distance.

I walked away from the grinning sergeant embarrassed but wiser.

Besides being a lesson for me, this was my first wake-up call. I felt I'd been caught with my pants down. The significance of that insignificant event was not lost on me. I saw it as a portent of the real situations I knew were soon to come.

I remained at Cam Ranh overnight and flew out in the morning on an Air Force C130 transport plane. We landed at Tan Son Nhut Airbase in Saigon. As we taxied, I could see splash marks (explosion scars that resembled splashes) on most concrete surfaces Weaker materials were penetrated through and through. The place had been hit hard during the recent TET offensive.

I flew again, ending up in the 90th Replacement Company at Long Binh, a short hop away. There I got assigned to the 25th Infantry Division, a seasoned combat unit. Once again I flew. This time to Cu Chi, the Headquarters of the 25th Infantry Division.

Cu Chi spread out as an expanse of sandbagged buildings in hues of beige. Metal roofs dotted the flat landscape under a grey sky alive with helicopters. Dust flew off its roads regularly as jeeps, trucks and armored personnel carriers drove by. The 25th Division patch painted boldly in front of its headquarters, depicted a crimson jungle leaf bordered in yellow, with a yellow thunderbolt in the middle. That patch adorned everyone's left shoulder here at Cu Chi and the surrounding bases. I thought that at the very least, I would be with the guys who wore what I considered the best-looking patch of all the units in Vietnam.

The guys here appeared harder than the guys I'd seen in Cam Ranh. Those had been administrative and clerk types. I'd soon hear their type referred to as REMFs. REMF was a derogatory term in Vietnam. It stood for Rear Echelon Mother Fucker. Combat soldiers often used it when referring to soldiers with safe duty in rear areas. Some, however, served in the relative safety of Cu Chi because they'd spent too much time in combat. Many had been given safer duties because of serious wounds they'd sustained out in the field. I met one such individual my first day...

Another commonly used acronym was FNG. I hated that term the first time I heard it and would for the rest of my life. I was easy to identify as an FNG (Fucking New Guy) as I shuffled around in rumpled, un-faded jungle fatigues. Usually, the dark olive color of these uniforms faded after a few washings as did the stigma associated with them.

FNG's like me milled about stirring up the red dust that was one of Cu Chi's hallmarks. We'd been here for a day or so to attend the mandatory five-day Jungle Warfare School. At some point of downtime, a small, rumpled man approached me. His approach was casual. He asked if I was new. I knew he already knew the answer. His fatigues fit him better than mine did. Faded green and worn creases complemented by rank and combat patches told much about him. His shoulders carried some invisible weight. His weariness preceded him.

"Just get here?" He asked.

"Yeah," I answered, eying his insignias.

We fell into a conversation easily. My anxious questions got answered with deliberate ease. His demeanor was soothing. He sought to assure and prepare me. One sequence of our conversation froze his image and etched his words into my consciousness with a permanent, perfect clarity.

"Have you ever gotten wounded?" I asked.

"I got shot six times."

He stood stoic through my stunned and surprised reaction. I felt dwarfed. The fear of being a green, new guy developed in me once again.

"How could you stay alive after getting shot six times?"

He lifted his shirt and showed me the scars from the bullets.

"Hell," he said, "A man's like a deer. You gotta hit him just right to kill him."

I still think of, and wonder about, that guy.

3

MPs, Rockets and the Firebase

Cu Chi bored me despite the temporary safety it offered me. That boredom caused thought and reflection which in turn snowballed into more premonition and fear. I felt a countdown going on within myself. No matter what I thought of this boring place, every minute in it was safe (or so I thought) and every minute that passed brought me closer to my ultimate assignment and mayhem. Grunt, 11 Bravo, Light Weapons Infantryman, whatever you called it, it all boiled down to the same thing. I was a basic foot soldier and I was about to face my enemy inexperienced. The 98th replacement company had sent me here and I knew this was the last stop before the bush. I wondered if I was a replacement for a dead guy or a survivor going home. A few more orientations and I would be in combat. I was scared. I was just a kid. We had some free time that evening so I walked around Cu Chi and then to the enlisted men's club. I'd just found this place the night before. Cold beer in refrigerated cases lay ahead of me just behind that door. Visions of cold glass bottles and bar stools distracted me till I saw the sign on the door: "Closed Till Further Notice." The refrigeration system had broken down. Disappointment and resignation blurred any direction I had when I started walking again.

Absentmindedly, I strolled a straight line through the thickest clusters of hooches in my view. Common sense indicated that I'd most likely find something to see or do there. The afternoon had given way to evening, and darkness settled around the base. In the drab, taupe-grey surroundings, a sign beamed bold letters on a white background, 25th Military Police Co. Not too far behind it, I heard men conversing and the clink of billiard balls. My spirit lifted. This meant entertainment and probably beer! Despite my fear of and distaste for MP's, I walked

M113 Armored Personnel Carrier at Cu Chi.

carefully towards that sound. I stood there and looked around for a while because I wasn't sure I should pass through this place. Then I realized that I had nothing to hide and I kept walking. Besides, there was no indication of anything telling me to stay out of there. Up ahead sat the hooch the sounds were coming from. It obviously served as some sort of recreational room. When I got to it I cocked my head in the doorway and asked a guy in a t-shirt, bent over a pool table, if I might enter and get a beer. I was given wary looks but another one of the guys inside eyed me carefully and in a silky voice said, "Sure, come in."

I have to say something here, risk of offense be damned. Because of the nature of their job of policing soldiers, MP's were generally disliked. They were among the most arrogant, aggressive, and condescending people in the Army. The only people that thought much of MP's were other MP's and higher-ranking officers who needed them to act as their control mechanism. MP's got into skirmishes with the enemy here and there and they occasionally escorted convoys, but generally speaking, they were noncombatant, rear echelon soldiers who drove around in jeeps and manned checkpoints. In basecamps, they were a nuisance. People in the rear areas knew the traps to avoid but the unpolished, unsuspecting combat soldier sent to the rear for illness, leave or any other reason at all was always a prime target for them. All it took was not having proper insignia, needing a shave or any other minor infraction. They always approached with menacing, predatory eyes. They were a pain in everyone's ass.

Stepping through that doorway felt good. I had belonged to no place in particular: a man with no place to go. Having a place to go, and something to do, felt good.

"You shoot pool?" One of them asked.

"Sure," I answered. "Can I buy a beer off you guys?"

He silently pointed at a large container with his cue stick.

"You play Eight Ball?" he asked.

"Yup" I replied.

I did play Eight Ball. In fact, I played it quite well. Having spent a large part of my youth in smoky pool halls throughout New York City, I was better at the game than most people in the Army. These guys had an assignment that allowed for plenty of recreational time. Unlike soldiers in the field, they got to play plenty of pool and were good at it by repetition and practice. They were not, however, as good as I.

As is typical in the military, a friendly game of pool quickly escalated into competition and wagering. Hunched over the green felt, I shot better than my opponents, and my winnings mounted with every cue stroke. Money had not changed hands yet with my current opponent. We tallied winnings and losses as we played. I crouched, lining my eye up with the cue tip and the ball I was aiming at when rockets came screaming in.

The walls shook from the first explosion. Immediately, everyone was in motion. The intense concentration of the game blinked away to sudden panic. Men charged through the hooch door and I ran after them. Their bunker stood close by and we ran into it. More huge explosions shook us. We were close enough to get killed, I thought, as we huddled in the bunker.

One at a time we left the bunker when it was over. I made my way back to the recreation hooch and was told that the gameplay had been interrupted, and therefore, I had forfeited my winnings. I was outnumbered by cops and protesting was useless. I'd won some money but the stakes had been raised significantly in the last games and there was no reason not to pay up. I walked away dejectedly disliking MP's all the more. I headed back to my assigned area and called it a night. Along the way, I passed wide-eyed soldiers talking about rockets. Smoke permeated the night air. The smell got stronger as I neared my barracks. I couldn't see much but there was no mistaking the acrid odor. Chemical and bitter, it lingered in my throat and nostrils. It fit well with my imagination's conjured images of danger and death. Then it faded as I neared my hooch. A rocket had hit close by. I was going to find out where in the morning.

The next morning, after chow, I kept my ears open for talk about the rockets. Sunlight warmed the top of my head right through my hat. The absence of clouds or wind created a mood as flat and still as the day. Soon I overheard that a rocket had hit by the enlisted men's club the night before. Trying not to be too obvious by running, I turned away and hurried over there.

The impact crater from the rocket explosion lay halfway between me and the EM Club. It was twenty-five feet away from me when I noticed it. I walked up to it and stared. Bending to a crouch, I ran my fingers through the gaping hole in the dirt. I felt a sharp edge and instinctively knew it was shrapnel. I retrieved it. In my palm, sunlight glinted off a jagged piece of steel the size of a half-dollar. Its surprisingly sharp edges could have cut my finger. The warhead of this rocket had been torn apart at the molecular level by explosive expansion speeds of approximately four miles per second. Lifting my head, I scanned the ground from the crater to the building. About thirty-five feet away lay the corner of the EM Club. Pockmarks were clearly visible on two walls. I walked over to take a closer look. Black holes peppered the building. Metal fragments had flown through wood as easily as if it were paper. On my left stood the door to the building. Not really thinking it was open, I tried the door anyway. To my surprise, it swung open.

I entered the dim interior of the club and froze. Before my eyes could adjust to the darkness, I saw the unbelievable. From all sides of the club, shafts of light shot crazily in all directions like laser beams. Standing there transfixed, I realized the significance of the light. Shrapnel had flown at hypervelocity in straight trajectories through these walls just like these beams of light. Scanning the room I realized that the bar, tables, and chairs were all riddled with holes. Had the club been open the night before, many people would have been killed and injured. Though I didn't consciously will it, I could hear the thought loudly: I would have been one of them. At that moment, I decided to buy a camera at the PX to begin documenting, when possible, the extraordinary things I knew I would see here.

In-country school ended and we got our final assignments. My name was on a list of 38 soldiers assigned to combat duty. As it turned out, approximately one out of six of us would die: most within the first two months. I know because years later I looked at my records and matched them against the Vietnam Wall.

My assigned unit was B Co., 2/12th Inf. Their base camp was at Dau Tieng to the north, but they were presently at a fire support base in the jungle. I was issued an M16 rifle and put on a helicopter headed there.

Flying in a helicopter fills the senses. From the forward tilt at take-off to the lift and forward momentum, nothing compares. Up, up, up, the air is cleaner and sweeter than any air I'd ever smelled. The door is open and wind swirls through my clothes, even through my pockets and underwear. The fabric of the clothes on my body rattles and sways to a windy beat slightly out of sync with that of the rotors. Everyone's hair flies wildly. The pilots face forward doggedly and their helmets hardly move. Gunners grip their machine guns in spellbound readiness. The ground falls further and further away. The steady rotor beat soothes passengers despite their fear of the destination. And so it was with me. I'd completed the in-country jungle school and was on my way to an infantry unit in the jungle, at their firebase. Tension tugged at my gut.

The M16 rifle cradled against my leg offered some comfort. The black, metal and plastic weapon exuded a tangible power. Having already fired hundreds of rounds through M16s in training, I was familiar with the rifle. I watched the landscape below me slide backward. If I looked hard enough, I could make out details on the ground. Impact craters from artillery and other ordnance dotted the landscape as far as I could see. Above me, the blur of the helicopter's blades grayed the blue sky as their constant wind cooled me. I relished these last pleasant moments. The relative safety of Cu Chi lay miles behind me. Ahead of me lay some of these closest brushes with death I would ever have.

Looking down, I regretted the descent as soon as it began. We'd come in fast over the treetops and drifted down onto the outpost in the middle of the jungle. It was less than a quarter of a mile in diameter; 105mm artillery pieces spiked outward inside the coiled barbed-wire perimeter. Ungainly armored personnel carriers sat near the wire with their machine guns pointed outward. Scattered everywhere were small tents and ragtag canvas enclosures. Squat little sandbagged squares dotted the place. Crude fighting positions made of metal culverts and sandbags ringed the base. The living conditions here were cruder than any slum or primitive campsite I'd ever imagined. It all resembled some post-apocalyptic scene right out of the movies.

As we landed, a sergeant ran up to the helicopter. Holding his jungle hat against his head and ducking against the wind, he yelled over the whine of the helicopter's rotors.

"New guy?" he asked.

I replied with a nod, as I ducked and moved away from the helicopter.

"Follow me." He replied as he beckoned with one hand.

I followed him to an area on another side of the base. It took less than ten minutes for cursory instructions. A piece of hard ground was assigned as my sleeping spot and I was pointed to an ammo bunker to get whatever I needed.

Once inside the squat bunker, I had to turn back around and push the canvas flap at the entry open again to get enough light to see. I turned and in the dim light, I saw crate after crate of grenades, high explosives, bullets, explosive projectiles, and every other type of ordnance. A childish feeling crept over me, I felt like a kid in a candy store. Having always been a fan of fireworks and explosions, I felt a delight opening crates to see what was in them. Every few boxes or so I'd find a new surprise. Here was C-4. There was TNT. This way was detonating cord. That way was fuse. Against a far wall, I found thermite grenades. This was the room of my dreams. All these years later, I'd still like to have some of that stuff.

As a kid, I loved firecrackers, bombs, and pyrotechnics. We'd take packs of firecrackers apart and meticulously empty all the powder from them to make one large firework. We measured our success by the loudness of the explosion we could create. The ultimate bragging right came from being able to truthfully say that our explosion made the cops come. My friends and I did it quite well and often. Now I was surrounded by the stuff of my dreams as a kid. As I read each wonderful new label, I'd grab more items and stuff my pockets. I left that bunker with fragmentation grenades, bullets, C-4, Flex-X sheet explosive, and a Claymore mine. When I came out of the bunker the sergeant eyed me up and down, shook his head slightly, and spoke with a wry grin. "Boy, if you get hit, you're goin' up like a Roman candle. They'll ship what's left of you home in a sardine can."

He laughed and walked away. I turned, went back to the ammo bunker, and put half the stuff back. I came back out, slightly embarrassed, and was met with quizzical, amused stares from my new platoon members. I walked over to my spot and sat staring at the tall jungle growth a hundred yards from the edge of the wire. Right behind that jungle growth, the enemy watched us. We'd go out to search for him from this temporary forward base. He'd constantly shift his position and shell us with rockets and mortars or ambush us. When we found him, we'd kill him or call air support to kill him. Then we'd look for more like him.

This was it. This was as bad as it got. The year was 1968 and I was a foot soldier in the worst war in the world: Vietnam.

4

Total Darkness and Explosions

I haven't been at the fire support base long; about a day and a half. It is a busy place. Soldiers mill about. Groups of them come in through the razor wire that is the perimeter; some leave through it. I've already been on an uneventful platoon-sized patrol myself. The constant boom of outgoing artillery fire here jars the senses and still startles me. Helicopters come and go with troops or supplies.

The base sits in the middle of the jungle. It is about four blocks wide and is ringed by razor wire. As busy as this place is, it is desolate and boring. I've met a handful of guys but they're not eager to socialize. They gather in small cliques and there is no telling where they disappear to when they leave the area. Now, as I look around I see only a few guys. They are huddled near a sandbag bunker. I'm new so I haven't been invited to hang with them yet. It gives me an empty feeling added to the already desolate feel of this place.

I'd been lying on my stomach so I roll over onto my side, propping my head up with my hand. My right hand feels the dead matted grass around me. This is my entire world: rifle, web gear, inflatable mattress, and half a metal culvert that is supposed to be some impromptu shelter in an attack or barrage. No matter how many times I think about it, I cannot imagine it protecting me from anything but rain. I am also concerned that the semi-circle of it surrounding me outlines me as a target. I reach over and feel its thickness between my fingers. I decided it could stop shrapnel from the sides as long as it wasn't too powerful. Crawling into it, I try it on for size. I crawl forward on the palms of my hands and then my elbows. I stop when most of my torso is surrounded by its metal. I look around and forward. If I position myself just right, I have a view of my section of the perimeter and the jungle forward of it.

4. *Total Darkness and Explosions*

A few coils of barbed wire separate me from the jungle and the enemy that roams it. I crawl back out of the culvert and onto my air mattress. Golden tips of sunlight crown the treetops as the sun sets and I lie there staring at stars that are just beginning to come out. The green below the trees narrows into darker green and then black where all color loses itself to the twilight of the jungle.

This was my home for a year. I couldn't grasp the concept yet. I felt like a man new to prison. One who looks at the four walls and doesn't know what to do with his hands while he copes with the fear of what lies ahead. Changing positions did little to help my level of comfort and only added to the lonely feeling. There was no place to go, nothing to do. I decided to lie on my back. That was more comfortable than sitting cross-legged or propped up on my elbows. Stars shone brighter above me as the day faded. Voiced muted, but the tempo of artillery pounding increased. The stars above me thrust their light sharper. I could see them move in the sky from the rotation of the earth combined with my stillness on the air mattress. I nodded off into the comfort of sleep but fully woke with each artillery blast. The rhythm of war cradled me roughly and I began getting acclimated to it. I slept again and dreamt troubled dreams that would not linger into memory.

A slow awareness of someone next to me wakes me. A foot nudges the end of my air mattress and my body bounces. I notice the stars were gone.

"You're the new guy.... Grzesik, right? Get your stuff ready. You're going on ambush patrol with those guys." He pointed. Fifteen feet or so away from me about five guys stood talking. Some had equipment and weapons. I stood, grabbed my stuff, slung it over my shoulder, and joined them. I listened for instructions but got little. Mostly I just watched them and followed their lead. If I needed to know something, I was told.

"Someone check out the new guy." Heads turned my way. A man walked towards me. He assigned me a walking position and told me to make sure I kept up. First, the last vestiges of light faded above the treetops and sky by the approaching night. Then the stars, which had begun pinpointing the sky, disappeared behind clouds which arrived sometime while I catnapped. Facial features became hard to recognize and darkness enveloped us further as if oozing from the very earth itself. Before long, I had to concentrate to make out any facial features at all. My thoughts turned to the ambush patrol we were going on. How was this supposed to work? Getting from one point to another was a matter of navigating with a map and compass but the maps had been folded and tucked away along with the compasses. We had only our leader's instinct to guide us.

"Saddle up everyone, we're going through the wire in a few minutes." I had no idea who was talking to us. I knew for certain that "the wire" was a reference to the razor wire that ringed the base. The prospect of leaving its crude confines unsettled me.

Rifle bolts opened and closed as rounds were chambered. Following their lead, I grabbed the triangular foregrip of my M16 with my left hand, and with my right, I pulled back the bolt and let it slam shut. It rammed a 5.56 bullet into the chamber and I now had a functioning machine gun in my hand. The familiar sound lent some empowerment to my faded confidence.

"C'mon, new guy, we're moving." A voice announced flatly. In the dark, our group of six men gathered and formed into a column. We began walking towards the razor wire encircling the base. I almost bumped into the man in front of me when he stopped because the column had stopped moving. Up ahead the wire made dull clinking sounds, very much like wind chimes but rusty ones, as it was opened to allow us passage.

"Tell him to be careful." Someone said. "Someone in third platoon got burned bad by a trip flare yesterday." Indeed someone had. I'd seen him walking around with a large white bandage on his hand. A machine-gunner from another platoon had opened the wire incorrectly. He got severely burned when he triggered the flare it was booby-trapped with. It had been set by our own guys to prevent the enemy from creeping through the wire.

We slowly walked out and I heard the clinking sound again. Someone was closing the wire behind us. Soon all sound faded behind us and the only audible sounds were those of our feet padding softly and the rubbing, tapping sounds our equipment made as we walked. It seemed to me it was getting darker by the minute. I swiveled my head up to look at the sky and saw nothing. The overcast had blocked all starlight. I had trouble seeing the man in front of me when I looked back towards him.

Soon, our walking became more labored. The grass was taller now and while the pace was still easy, the footsteps we took became more tentative. Then, in a matter of fifty feet, we slowed considerably. I thought we were near the wood-line because a root caught the tip of my boot. I lurched into the man in front of me. Though he said nothing, I sensed his annoyance. The vegetation thickened with every foot we progressed, and the swishing, clinking sounds of soldiers and their equipment changed to a louder sound of lumbering men and thuds. I heard someone crash through jungle thicket in front of me and picked out the sound of his plastic rifle stock hitting something: perhaps a tree. Though I was new, I couldn't help but think the entire premise of this mission was flawed. If there was an enemy out here, he'd hear us from a distance. I thought about the guys back behind the wire. They'd be of little help to us in this blackness.

Branches whipped by my raised arm now. Some snapped back and hit me in the face. I stumbled into the man in front of me again and felt flush with embarrassment and fear because I was losing control of my own feelings. Dread gripped me harder by the minute. The guy in front of me stopped and whispered. "Hold on to a piece of my equipment if you can't see me." He sounded sincere and friendly. That comforted me. I grabbed the first piece of his rucksack my fingertips found and held it but it swayed back and forth as he walked. This threw my own staggering rhythm off and helped me very little. We continued plodding this way: me grabbing his pack when I thought I would lose sight of him and letting go when I thought I knew where he was. The jungle got thicker and thicker. I could no longer see anything. I lifted my hand in front of my face and saw nothing but an inky black.

We had slowed so much we were barely moving. Maneuvering through a wall of forest vegetation, fumbling, almost falling in this total darkness ... walking was becoming impossible. I could tell others felt the same way from the intense whispering up ahead of me. Finally, we stopped where the forest relented somewhat. I felt around and knew there was room to move.

A voice ahead of me grunted softly, "We're going to stop and set up here." Another guy said something about setting up the proper ambush position but I doubt anyone took him seriously. Our common unspoken thought was to get down and be silent. A quiet shuffling and then silence ensued. We slithered and backed up on our bellies to put equal space between each other, and other than that, hardly anyone moved for the rest of the night. I don't think we even put Claymore mines out that night even though they usually were a core piece of equipment in an ambush. We lay prone for the rest of the night. Hardly a word was said other than the few words exchanged with others during the change of watch.

We Had to Get Out of That Place

I lay prone for the rest of the night, sleeping on and off. When the time came, a watch was passed to me with a warning to not fall asleep on guard duty. The short period of nodding off provided some rest and an escape from the reality of my situation. This cycle repeated two or three times in the dark of the forest.

Towards morning a cold mist enveloped us. For a short while, I marveled at the sensation of cold and then it was gone as the grey light of morning sifted down around us from the tree-tops. The morning brought with it a relief for me. We all felt it, I'm sure. The trip back was easy because we could see where we were going, even though we were still in hostile territory.

When it was all over, I realized we'd only gone half a mile out of the wire. I walked back to my area exhausted.

The next day I woke from sleeping under the culvert section again. Again, as I crawled out from under it, I thought about how puny it was. I felt drained. I doubt I ever got more than two hours of sleep before being woken for some type of guard duty or by the nonstop thunder of the 105mm artillery pieces fired randomly all night long. The deafening sound made sleep impossible. I found myself fearing sleep because the deeper I slept the worse the effect of waking to those explosions was on the nerves. The ground I just spent the night on bears the scars of a thousand boots. The wood-line in the distance looks just as menacing as the night before. The enemy lurks somewhere beyond the first trees. Voices slowly rise in volume in the morning dusk. I see guys in small groups eating morning C rations.

I've never felt so alone in my life. I am a new guy, but not just any new guy, I am a brand-new-in-Vietnam, new guy. I've been referred to as an FNG, though rarely to my face. My factory new, dark olive uniform gave me away to everyone. It had not been worn thin or bleached by the sun yet. I stood out, too new to make any friends for now. Nobody here likes new guys and everyone outside the firebase wants to kill me. I feel more accepted out on combat patrols because there, silence rules, and I fit in as a cog in the machine as it grinds its deadly work. I have to take the initiative because I've been here several days and still haven't talked to anyone for any length of time. At some point, I will have to because no one is reaching out to me. Bolstering my courage, I stand up and walk over to the guys squatting or sitting in groups eating chow. "Where can I get some C rations," I ask the guy closest to me as I approach the group.

"Over there. If there's not a full box, crack a new case." He points with a white plastic spoon towards a clutter of C ration cases.

I walked over and returned with a box of "Beefsteak and Potatoes with Gravy" and stood among the guys.

"You a Yankee? You sound like a Yankee." Another one of the guys I had just spoken to smiles as he chides me. His smile is genuine though it is more of a smirk.

"Yeah, I'm from New York City," I answer. "Oh, we got us a real Yankee" someone else chimes in. "Well, I'm George, a proud Southern boy by the grace of God. Sit down and take a load off." He also points with his spoon and I sit down in the dirt. We spoke little as we ate. Then George looked up at me and told me I didn't have to sleep alone in the culvert and away from everybody every night.

With that, I felt the first hint of ease and began breaking the ice and introducing myself to a few of the guys. Sunny, morning air buoyed my spirits. I walked my platoon's area with a lighter step and a more positive attitude. As I meandered through small groups of men a voice boomed behind me, "Platoon meeting now!"

All heads turned towards the voice. Men began standing. Some muttered blurbs of disapproval and a stream of bodies converged as a group to the area the voice had come from. Everyone sat down in a rough circle. A single man in the group spoke out.

"Good morning men. How y'all doin'?" He slid on his butt further towards the center of the circle and looked around at all of us.

He was our platoon leader. A young lieutenant, his freshness stood out in his sparkling honest smile. Piercing blue eyes twinkled as he spoke. He could have been any kid just several years ahead of my senior class. I could tell by his drawl that he hailed from some southeast corner of the United States. There was a boyishness about him that told me he lived in the country. There was none of the jaded big-city quality that some people called sophistication.

Then he spoke again. "Later this afternoon we're going out and setting up an ambush overnight." Then he smiled broadly and said with delight, "Gentlemen, we're going to get a body count."

A feeling of cold dismay spread from my stomach outward and then throughout my body. It was not what he said as much as how he said it. This was war and I knew that. We've been taught all about this in training and I was under no illusions, yet here it was presented in cold, sober words that jarred me almost as much as the reality could. I could not believe that he felt about this the way he had sounded while announcing it. Perhaps this was a leadership mechanism to motivate men and keep them rooted in reality. Then I realized that my reaction to his words was probably just what he wanted.

It didn't take long for the gravity of my situation to begin slowly gnawing away at me again. Interludes of lighthearted conversation happened only occasionally. The rest of the time we functioned as soldiers in war. I would be shot at and people would try to kill me for almost a year.

I'd taken to distracted daydreaming. Retreating into comforting thoughts dulled the boredom and fear. When not busy, men's minds often wandered to fear or daydreaming. In Vietnam survival depended on alertness, and our leaders always demanded it. Feeling some measure of security behind our barbed wire, with the sun on my neck, my mind wandered as my boots crunched softly on the worn grass of the firebase. All I had to worry about were rockets, mortars and the location of a hole to jump into if I heard them landing. There had been no such incident since the rocket attack at Cu Chi and my ease suddenly shattered as I heard someone bellow, "Fire in the hole."

Less than a second passed. I had ducked and was still looking for a trench or hole to jump into when a terrific explosion jolted me.

The ground moved beneath my feet and I felt the thump of a massive explosion. Disoriented, I staggered and thought that the sky had turned dark. I looked up and it was true. The blue of the sky was gone. It was black. After a second of confusion, I realized I was looking at blasted matter blown high into the air above me. Having no place to run, I danced back and forth like some outfielder desperate to catch a ball. In my case the opposite was true. I was desperate not to catch what was coming down. Lines of light and cracks of sky formed all over the wall of blackness above me. The cracks grew bigger and soon they overtook the dark matter in size and shape. Now I was running around trying to avoid the huge chunks of matter that were about to hit the ground around me. I was successful. Clumps of dirt thudded harmlessly to the ground around me. None of them hit me. It was over. I stood there in stunned amazement as the last remnant of the debris, a mild sandstorm, gently floated down onto me. I found out later that the blast was an attempt to find groundwater. The demolition guys had simply dug a hole and detonated a large canister of ammonium nitrate explosive in it. They placed little importance on the timing of the mandatory "fire in the hole" warning.

4. Total Darkness and Explosions

A few weeks later, my second encounter with the demolition guys would be more hair-raising than the first.

We'd been walking for hours and had made no enemy contact. Our shirts were wet and our faces glistened with sweat as a humid, hot Vietnamese afternoon descended on us like a weight. The company commander stopped the operation we had been conducting and ordered us to set up a defensive perimeter among unused enemy foxholes we had found. This was not unusual and we did it often because abandoned foxholes or fighting positions provided instant cover if needed. A Viet Cong crept up as close as he could without being seen and fired a full magazine of AK-47 bullets at us. We all scrambled for cover. By the time we were ready to deal with him, he was gone. The CO then moved us into the edge of the rubber plantation. We walked for half an hour and arrived at some strategic point in the plantation the captain had picked. My platoon had not set up yet and I stood there between rubber trees in the gloom keeping watch.

"Fire in the Hole," yelled a demolition man. I whirled in time to see the flash and thunder of a block of C4 explosive blowing one of the rubber trees. It was done so the mortar men could have an unobstructed firing position, but it was done without enough warning. The tree shattered and a large part of it flew straight towards me. Time slowed down and the sequence unfolded in slow motion because of my shock at what I was seeing. It seemed as though there were three stages to what occurred. First the flash and the separation of the splintering trunk in various directions with the largest piece coming my way. Then, the visual of it looming only several feet from my face. In the nick-of-time, I ducked and avoided it slamming into my face as it whizzed by me. I estimated it was at least two feet long and six inches thick at its widest point. It would have killed me or, at the very least, seriously injured me if it had hit me.

I felt a flash of anger at the demolition guy before I turned and re-joined my men.

5

Mortars and Prisoners

We're out on another patrol again. I have no idea where we are. The sun is just beginning to sink towards the horizon. Bright greens close to me have faded to olive, and if I look up, leaves are silhouetted black spots against a sky that is turning shades of red and yellow. Over my shoulder, the sky has turned a deep blue with a sprinkling of stars. Ahead of me, I can see the green jungle begin to dim to darker shades, heralding the night and its apprehensions. We've been walking longer than usual and I'm surprised we haven't stopped because of the encroaching darkness. We are usually set up by now to avoid walking into an ambush. Just then our column slows.

Up ahead people are taking off their gear and I assume that we have arrived at our destination. We have walked upon a clearing with foxholes dug all over its perimeter. My guess is that these were dug by North Vietnamese Army troops. They are precise rectangles, all the same size and equidistant to each other. One of our officers decides this is a good place to set up for the night. We don't know it yet but we are being watched.

We begin the usual routine of setting up a night defensive position. I place my equipment near one of these holes, making sure my grenades and ammunition are the easiest to reach. The next thing we will do is go forward of the position to set out Claymore mines.

We hear the sound in the distance, "Thoomp Thoomp Thoomp." The sound is similar to a magnum champagne bottle being uncorked at a distance, but much deeper. Everyone freezes and all heads turn to look at each other as one man has the presence of mind to yell, "Mortars!"

Somewhere in the distance, probably half a mile away or more, a man is dropping explosive, rocket-like projectiles into a leaning tube. When they hit the bottom, an explosive charge sends them flying out of the tube in a high arc to eventually descend on our position. They are packed with explosives, detonate on impact, and can easily kill a man from twenty to fifty yards depending on their size.

I dive into the hole I am next to. A second later another guy dives on top of me. My legs are shaking and I am glad to have his weight and cover over me. A few seconds later we hear the hiss of the mortars in the air. A second after that the first one hits. Then, multiple equally spaced large explosions rip the night air. At one point they are getting closer to me and then further away. I wonder if there are any men stuck on the bare ground outside my hole.

The attack stops and we climb out of our holes. Everyone is quiet. We are listening intently to hear if any more tubes are going off in the distance. Then we quickly set up the rest of the night defensive perimeter because an attack after the mortar barrage is very possible. Almost nothing is said that night and everyone stays on high alert. By dawn, as light starts filtering through the jungle, we begin to feel more at ease. If they haven't attacked us yet they most probably won't now.

The order comes to move out of there and we hurry to do so. It is apparent the enemy knows exactly where we are. Within minutes we are walking again. As we leave, I look around. It is light enough now to discern our surroundings. I can see the line of explosion splash scars left in the dirt by the mortars. They "walked them in" on a straight line right through our position.

Amazingly, no one was wounded. We began walking again and soon we are among rubber trees at the edge of the jungle. As I plod along, I'm grateful we're not in that primordial forest anymore. The jungle is thicker on the edges of the rubber plantation; as if nature deliberately grew back the foliage in a frenzy where it was cleared. I have learned to recognize red ant nests. Leeches are harder. Most of the time we don't see them until they are clearly visible on someone's body. "Hey man, you've got a leech on you." I've heard that several times. We have long-sleeved shirts for protection, but we usually roll up the sleeves because of the heat. My forearms are scarred from the bamboo I have walked through. It has sharp spurs coated with blackish grime. Sometimes the cuts get infected. Mostly they just bleed. Our shirts are made of rip-stop poplin so they usually remain intact.

The neat rows of rubber trees give the illusion of civility. They appear carefully manicured and equidistant from each other. Also, the plantation always feels cooler than the jungle. Nonetheless, it is hot, too hot. We march one foot in front of the other. There is little to look at but

I scan the area around me. The rest of the time I'm looking at the gear of the guy in front of me. Somewhere up ahead there is a commotion. All heads look up and forward. We all see them. Two men on bicycles with AK-47 rifles wave at us. Everyone is bewildered by the sight. One man rallies his senses and raises his rifle to shoot, but a lieutenant pushes his rifle barrel down with the palm of his hand. The two cyclists drop their bicycles and run into the jungle while we all raise our weapons to fire after them. My own rifle jams and I watch a few guys run after them. Booming voices stop them for fear of being drawn into an ambush.

While I rarely knew where we were operating in relation to our base-camp in Dau Tieng or the firebase, the Michelin rubber plantation was always recognizable. Rows of neatly planted rubber trees, with diagonal sap collection cuts, stretch as far as the eye can see to a perfect vanishing point, the kind I'd learned about during art class in high school. The plantation was built by the Michelin company in 1925. At 31,000 acres and twenty miles at the widest point, it is the largest rubber plantation in Vietnam. It is located approximately halfway between the Cambodia border and Saigon and is used extensively as a staging area for the North Vietnamese coming off the Ho Chi Minh trail beyond the Cambodian border. Dau Tieng sat between the Michelin and Ben Cui rubber plantations.

The Michelin was the first place I ever got shot at and patrolling it was rarely uneventful. Often we walked the perimeters of it instead of the internal areas. My guess was that bad guys infiltrated and escaped later from the jungle on the peripheries of it. Often we encountered civilians working in the rubber. We'd always approach them with great caution. The Vietcong often dressed in civilian clothes and civilians themselves could easily be enemy sympathizers.

The next day, we are patrolling again in the Michelin. A bead of sweat runs off my forehead and into my eye. It rolls quickly as it follows the moist trail left by the last drop. I squint. My eye stings and I wipe it with the left sleeve of my jungle fatigues. It is too damn hot. Here on the edge of the rubber plantation where rubber trees fade into jungle, sunlight mottles the ground around us because the leaves above us were not yet dense enough to stop it. Looking further through the scrub I can see where it gets darker and thicker. Beyond that lies Charlie's domain: triple canopy jungle with layer upon layer of overlapping tree-tops. Little light makes it to the jungle floor there, and seeing through the multiple canopies from the air is impossible. For that reason, the enemy loves the jungle; and though it hides him well, we were getting better and better at finding him there. The tide is turning.

I squint again to see farther into the indiscernible darkness when I hear an approaching vehicle. Whirling, I look towards the sound. A white truck is approaching us parallel to our column. Acting on sheer instinct, I leap out between my guys and the approaching truck. Out of the corner of my eye, I see a black guy from one of the other platoons run out as well. The truck passes him and heads my way. I raise my arm in a high arcing wave.

"Dung lai," I bellow at the top of my voice. It meant "stop" in Vietnamese.

The motor of his ancient truck screams as he accelerates. The son-of-a-bitch is trying to get away. I can see the driver clearly. He does not look at me. He looks straight ahead with dogged determination as he speeds past me.

"Dung lai," I scream again as I raise my rifle and aim at the passing truck.

He is moving away even faster now. I squeeze the trigger, my sights align with the quickly fading truck. Multiple bullets streak out of my rifle in an automatic burst. At the same time, the black dude fires his M79 grenade launcher off to my right. He knows the truck was getting away and in his haste, he never aimed properly. His angle is too shallow. The projectile leaves the barrel of his weapon in a loud "thoomp," and hits the ground halfway between me and the truck. The explosion flashes thirty feet away from me and shrapnel whizzes by me but misses me. Meanwhile, the truck had skidded to a stop. Carefully, the black guy and I inch our way towards the truck, he on the passenger's side, I on the driver's side. I grab the door handle and yank it open. Inside sit two Vietnamese men, shaking uncontrollably in fear. As I grab the driver and yank him out, I see three bullet holes perfectly stitched in the metal above the windshield where the tops of their heads had been. All eyes in the column are on me, a new guy, as I self-consciously march my prisoner back to be interrogated.

Unbelievably, only a couple of days passed before I had another such incident. On this particular day, my company moved through the rubber trees somewhere on the inside of the plantation. We moved parallel to a road because that gave us some cover and concealment among the rubber trees. Walking directly on the road would have made us an easy target, even from a distance.

We Had to Get Out of That Place

We'd been walking for an hour and had run into no one on the road or in the rubber trees when I heard a motor vehicle coming from our rear. I'd been walking flank on the side of the column as usual so I was the first one to react. Stepping off to my left, I crouched to conceal myself and watched a truck approach. When it was about a hundred feet away from me, I jumped out into the road and waved my arms and rifle at the driver to stop him. At first he didn't slow down so I took a chance and stepped out further to the middle of the road and yelled "Dung Lai." I stood there in that red dirt with my chest puffed out determined to make him stop. Everyone in my company had heard the commotion and all eyes were upon me. The truck stopped ten feet in front of me and the driver got out. Next, a small child and a younger man exited the truck cab. Clenching my rifle, I looked at the driver's face and saw he was sweating profusely. His short-sleeved shirt gleamed lily white and clean. It was clear to me this was some type of professional man because he certainly was not a rubber worker. I noticed more beads of sweat were forming on his forehead. His passenger looked poorly dressed compared to him and I felt a tinge of suspicion.

By this time my guys were approaching and they surrounding us. I pointed to the ground to communicate to the men from the truck not to move, and to my surprise, the elder guy replied "OK" distinctly and clearly, catching me off guard. I began examining the contents of the truck's cab. There was nothing. The truck was empty except for a single sheet of paper in the cab, printed in Vietnamese.

Figuring White Shirt knew some English, I walked up and confronted him. "What's this?"

"Menu-restaurant-Saigon," he replied.

Legitimate, I thought. No reason to hold them up anymore. I even felt a bit disconcerted because by this time the child was frightened and crying. This man looked like a solid citizen, well dressed, and probably a regime loyalist from the upper class.

I was about to let them all go when I saw another group of our soldiers approach us. With them was an ARVN interpreter I hadn't seen before. He was handed the sheet of paper by a lieutenant. After scanning it briefly, he looked up at us. "This paper medical supplies. This man Viet Cong."

We took them all prisoner. The child's screams rang in my ears as they were led off.

I would go on to have other encounters in the Michelin rubber plantation and though I did not know it yet, later in life I would replay these events over and over again in my mind. As I grew older, I questioned the other possible outcomes my actions could have had. What if I had shot two young men in the truck for no reason? Men who were simply trying to get away from what they perceived to be a danger. What if the Vietnamese authorities that we turned them over to beat or tortured them during their interrogation? The soldiers on bicycles we'd opened up on might have been crippled for life if our bullets had hit them. Maybe, they actually did hit them. I imagined them bleeding out in the heat, on the jungle floor with insects buzzing over their flowing blood. In future years, the further I was from those events, the more I would question them. Broken bodies, broken men. All for a noble cause unfulfilled.

6

War Dog Twice

Everything that happened from the moment we arrived on that mission eclipsed its inconsequential beginnings. The following events are etched in my memory. They may have occurred on a different time-line. I cannot remember. These incidents occurred over forty-four years ago, in a sleep-deprived, stressed state. One thing I do remember is meeting that dog—the hard way.

I was still very new in-country and that fact was obvious to everyone around me. A lot of the old-timers looked older than I did even though they weren't. They had cynical, sunken eyes. When they spoke their words were often tinged with sarcasm. Black humor was their favorite. For the most part, I was treated respectfully but I could sense that I was being tolerated, but still not fully accepted.

Night had fallen at the firebase and I had to relieve myself. I thought I'd just walk out towards the wire, do my business and come back. But, when returned, I was stopped by a deep-throated growl and a glowing set of teeth. The scout dog appeared before me and was about to tear me to pieces before his handler leaped out of the darkness and restrained him in the nick of time. He stood there and lectured me about what that dog could have done to me, and how I should let somebody know if I was going forward of our perimeter.

I'd have another encounter with that dog soon enough.

That week I flew on my first Eagle Flight combat assault. As usual, the word trickled down the chain of command to put our gear on for another mission. Usually, the blast of heat that drenched us in sweat didn't start till later in the day. That morning it hit hard the second we stepped out from under the rubber plantation's cooling leaves, and it blazed hot the rest of the day.

After putting on our gear, we met up at the helicopter landing zone and positioned ourselves to walk in two columns. Most guys carried extra water and equipment. The little bit of info I got on the mission was from our machine-gunner. He'd simply answered, "Eagle Flight" with an arrogant, knowing smile when I asked if he knew where we were going. "Eagle Flight" was a euphemism in the 25th division for a combat assault carried out by waves of helicopter formations.

Pale blue sunny skies illuminated the long dark strip cleared in the deep green wood-line. This was either the runway at Dau Tieng or simply a clearing by a wood-line suitable for aviation approaches. I can't remember. Our two columns split to either side of it. People were temporarily removing their heavy gear. We'd packed extra gear and walked a while to get here. "Don't get too comfortable," someone yelled, "Birds are en route to our location."

Soon, a distant hum gathered in strength and momentum. It increased to a rhythmic roar as the first wave of UH-1H helicopters descended on us. Olive drab birds, with unit insignia on their noses, gently bumped the earth as they landed. Our men struggled aboard under the weight of their gear. They crouched and held their helmets to their head with a free hand as they rushed to their respective choppers. A sudden roar, increasing in intensity, marked the takeoff as the pilots

"Eagle Flight" formation of helicopters taking troops into combat.

gunned their engines. Simultaneously, the choppers took off in a synchronized forward tilt and lift. The formation of helicopters flew off and soon another came to take its place. Too soon, it was my turn to climb into a bird and sit on the floor till it rose with me. The floor of the bird pressed up beneath me as we lifted.

The world outside the door of the helicopter skewed as it pitched and disoriented my perspective. Trees dropped away beneath us and we turned to look at each other. Some guys avoided eye contact by looking down at the floor or out the door of the bird. As we flew a calm came over me. The air rushing through the open doors had an air conditioning effect. But for the tension I felt, I could have fallen asleep. Beating blades and the drone of the engine soothed me. Although it was only my second or third flight in a helicopter, it felt like the best one. I found myself hoping the ride was a long one because I felt like an inmate on his last walk before entering a dangerous dark place. I knew that the pleasant breezes in the helicopter were temporary and that very soon we'd be landing in that dark dangerous place. The unspoken question was, what situation were we flying into? I'd heard about hot LZs (landing zones) where soldiers took fire the moment they touched down or even while still in the air. To me, that was the equivalent of being a sitting duck. I closed my eyes.

All too soon, we descended for landing. The landscape got bigger as though we were looking at it through a zooming lens. The jungle rose towards us beckoning with a dark green that turned knots in my stomach. Someone in the bird pointed down. People jockeyed for position to get out of the helicopter as quickly as possible. When we touched down, the guys sitting in the doorway jumped first. I slid across the floor and fell out onto the tall grass of the large clearing using my backpack as a cushion. I was one of the last ones out so I followed the others, in a lumbering jog, towards the edge of an ancient, dark jungle forest.

All of this had been preplanned by the commanding officer, his lieutenants, and platoon sergeants. Between hand signals and sharply spoken orders, everyone knew where to go. A few minutes after we passed under the first trees of the wood-line, daylight faded and the gloom of the jungle enveloped us. At the same time, rifle fire, punctuated by explosions, erupted in the distance to our right. One of our elements had just made contact with the enemy, and in a matter of seconds, was actively engaged in a full-blown firefight. All heads turned to people in charge and we were told to take cover. We all got down

Entering the jungle before a firefight.

and the captain was informed by radio that Charlie was moving towards us. Someone huddled down by my group and pointed into the forest. "They'll be coming from that way," he pointed. After some initial strategy emerged, our column moved off to the left and right. We formed a line abreast of each other and peered into the distance where the enemy was thought to be coming from.

I was fortunate enough to have a tree, about fourteen inches in diameter, near me. I lay down in the prone rifle position, behind it. Calculations ran through my mind as to which parts of the trunk could stop a bullet and where one could go through and hit me. I even thought that the outer edges could deflect a bullet or absorb enough energy from it to prevent it from killing me. I'd have to fight for the part of me that was exposed. They could only hurt me on the left and right side of my body and, if I fought hard enough, they wouldn't get the chance, I thought. This was my reasoning as I lay on that jungle floor staring into the green, listening to my heart thud. I could see only the depth of a tennis court before leaves and branches all blended into each other. The distance was too close for comfort. I'd seen this scenario in war movies as a kid. A Marine down in the dirt on Tarawa or Iwo Jima craning to see through the foliage. I'd always imagined my first firefight would be at some distance.

I lay there afraid. Who was I kidding? A bullet could go right through my tree. My intense concentration dulled my exterior senses. I heard artillery rounds impacting and they distracted me from concentrating on what might be coming in front of me. Then I smelled smoke. I'd been smelling it all along but because of the stress of the situation, I hadn't really noticed it. Bright blue billows of smoke churned around us and became strong and offensive. I turned, and in the distance saw more smoke curling through the trees with licks of flame behind it. I had no idea what ignited a fire in the forest I was lying in, but it occurred to me that I was sandwiched between two deadly situations: fire and North Vietnamese (or Vietcong) troops. I suppressed pulses of panic. Months of training paid off. I now understood what a favor those hated drill sergeants did us with their nonstop lectures in basic and advanced training. I thought of my own sergeant back in basic training...

Suddenly, I smelled stronger, choking smoke. Almost immediately, flames began crackling just to my rear, almost on top of us. We were given the order to move and snaked our way out of there, working between the flames. We regrouped near the wood-line we'd come in on and awaited further instruction. Confusion quickly turned to urgency as the captain ordered us to stack all our water and extra supplies there on the forest floor. We were going after the enemy, probably to relieve the guys in the firefight. Speed and mobility were of the essence.

Hours passed. Step after step, one tired foot in front of the other, we walked on. The fire flight had stopped and the jungle seemed too quiet. Stopping, searching, walking again; we found nothing. Smoke still hung in the air as we walked quickly but silently. I had no idea where the other unit was and the chaos of it all always concerned me.

I took another step and an orange-pink flash, eight feet in diameter, accompanied by a thunderclap, erupted in front of me almost knocking me to the ground. An RPG had slammed into a tree fifteen feet to my left front. I staggered backward. The explosion had smashed my shirt against my chest. I looked down to see if it was ripped. Amazingly, no shrapnel had struck me. A sergeant I disliked, already on the ground with everyone else, looked up at me with scorn and said, "Maybe now you'll learn to pay attention." Sgt. Ramirez and I had developed a mutual dislike for each other. It would become a problem for me. Later, he would get hit by a piece of harmless but painful shrapnel in the butt— poetic justice for a man that was a pain in the ass.

Surprisingly, only one person, the one closest to the explosion, got hit. Though he never made a sound, the platoon medic raced forward to check on him. It was our radioman. They both came back from the direction of the explosion with the radio operator wearing a smile. From directly under his left eyeball a single drop of blood rolled down his face. A piece of shrapnel had entered his eye socket with no apparent ill effect. He had what was referred to as the million-dollar wound. The medic's assessment was that specialized surgery in the States would be required to remove this piece of shrapnel before it migrated towards his brain or eyeball. His tour of Vietnam was over and he would be sent home with a Purple Heart.

As we lay on the ground, the word fanned out. An air strike was on the way. Those in dangerous proximity scrambled to safety. We quickly adjusted ourselves to positions of cover or sat down on the jungle floor and waited. Then we realized we were missing a guy: one who was almost deaf ... another one who had no business being in the Army. A sergeant barked that someone needed to go get him because he'd stayed behind, too close to the expected bomb impact area the rest of his men had just scrambled away from. Nobody went after him and soon we heard the approaching jet. The distant howl of its engine almost imme-diately turned into a loud whine and then a scream. I looked up just in time to see it come down and arc back up with a roaring, whooshing sound as it released its bomb. We all cast quick glances at each other before hugging the dirt with our bodies and faces.

The loud, crunching sound of the shock wave preceded the boom of the earth-shaking explosion. It felt as though I'd been lifted off the ground or it had fallen away from me. There was no doubt that the ground moved. I felt an earthquake-like sensation come through the ground into the core of my body. After a few seconds, we heard the thud of bomb fragments hitting the jungle all around us. A piece the size of a golf ball landed right next to the guy in front of me. He took his canteen out and poured water on it. He grinned at us as it sizzled and I stared in disbelief as steam rose from it.

We held our position for quite a while waiting, waiting. I'd been rationing what water I had left since we left our supplies in a heap near the LZ. My tongue and throat were drying, my voice and breath became raspy. At some point, we'd gotten the word that the enemy had cut us off from our supplies. Many guys were out of food and more importantly, water.

A corridor of sorts, perhaps a trail between the trees, scoped out through the jungle towards the direction of the bomb blast. It was our longest view towards the enemy position as well as the most dangerous place to stand and be exposed. Since animals and humans take the path of least resistance I concluded this was probably a well-used jungle trail.

I turned my head towards the sound of crunching boot steps behind me. Two of our experienced guys were being sent down the trail to do a reconnaissance. I was glad it wasn't me. They stepped lightly, their eyes and expressions strained, then they were gone. When they returned, half an hour later, they were both grinning. They'd found two shallow grave mounds and dug one up. They uncovered a dead enemy soldier, his arms crossed on his chest. The live enemy, however, was long gone. After a few minutes, we got up to pursue them. Darkness began to fall and a dangerous night was approaching. We found no sign of them. They had simply melted away into the jungle. We set up a defensive perimeter about sixty yards in diameter in a clearing we found. The enemy could be anywhere. They were probably watching us now. Darkness fell upon us before we were done getting set up. Meanwhile, I was getting thirstier and had no food or water left.

When the light began fading, the jungle's features melted into creeping shadows. We had to be ready for a night attack so we hurried to organize our positions while we could still see. Machine gunners placed their weapons and memorized their fields of fire. People opened their backpacks to have ready access to extra ammunition. High explosive Claymore mines were set well forward of the men. Their devastating power could stop a human wave attack and that was what they were invented for. They consisted of seven hundred steel balls embedded in a slab of C4 plastic explosive, all encased in a plastic shell with foldable legs that stuck in the ground. The mine, shaped like a curved rectangle, achieved a sixty-degree spread of the steel projectiles. They were most often used forward of night defensive positions. A blasting cap attached to a sixty-foot wire was inserted into it. On the other end was the hand-held electric generator the soldier used to detonate it. When detonated, the steel balls traveled at almost three thousand feet per second, the speed of a bullet. Claymore mines were used extensively in Vietnam.

That night we had them spiking out from all sides of our defensive position. The rest of the night was spent simply lying peering into the dark where imagined shadows turned into real shadows. Those shadows moved if you looked at them hard enough.

I knelt on the grass arranging my equipment and rucksack for the night so I could have ready access to everything. A sergeant approached me and said, "Grzesik, you and him go out there and set up a listening post." He pointed to another guy and then moved his finger towards the darkness. Listening post is simply a position of two or three men set well forward of the main position to listen for sounds in the night. My guess was there would probably be at least four listening posts around our perimeter. Again that helpless, vulnerable feeling descended upon me as I looked at the blackness I had to crawl into. My hand fished around in my pile of equipment till I found the bandoleer of ammo I usually wore on the outside of my web gear. It consisted of a sling holding seven M16 magazines, loaded with 20 bullets each. I wanted to travel as light as possible in case I had to scramble back to our position. Swinging it over my shoulder, I grabbed my rifle and thought about grabbing a grenade too, but I didn't like throwing them in total darkness. Scattered trees stood about a hundred feet from us. I was going to be much closer to them and I didn't want a live grenade bouncing off a limb and exploding too close to me. Grenades were timed to explode three seconds after being thrown and there was no way to stop the internal fuse once it was activated. Usually, I liked to wait half a second or so before throwing one to prevent it from immediately being thrown back.

My partner and I slithered out into the night on our stomachs. We could have quickly trotted out crouching, but we decided that minimizing any visible profile was the best idea. Fifty feet was far out enough from the perimeter that no one behind us could see us. We stopped. I waited for the words "Get further out," but thankfully, I never heard them. To this day I believe sending us out there was unnecessarily dangerous. Also, in this particular situation, we could have gotten shot by our own guys, since many of them probably didn't know we were out there. Again, I felt the futility of my situation. If a firefight erupted in the night, we could be shot at from both sides. We lay there quietly, not even whispering to each other. I hardly knew this guy anyway. I think we took turns napping and at some point in the night, I felt what I thought was a rock near my head. It felt smooth and concave so I rested my head in it.

I snapped alert and became focused on the sound of an approaching helicopter. The sound got louder and soon there were lights in the trees over my left shoulder. A large Chinook helicopter came over the wood-line from behind me and hovered over the middle of our night defensive position. It was there to re-supply us with water among other things. As it hung in the air and slowly turned, its front lights illuminating the area forward of it, a blast shattered the night off to my left. Almost simultaneously, I heard a piercing scream. It sounded inhuman and I assumed our scout dog had gotten hit by shrapnel. The remainder of the night kept me wide-eyed and shaken to the core. When daylight came I realized that the "rock" I'd been using as a pillow was actually a Claymore mine that I'd knocked over. Its detonation wire led back to our guys.

When we got back to the guys we were told that when the Chinook swung around, its lights caught a VC on the edge of the wood line with an RPG (Rocket Propelled Grenade) on his shoulder, ready to fire at the helicopter. Someone paying attention saw him and blew their Claymore. The scream I heard was the last sound that enemy soldier ever made in his life. He was found dead in the wood line, riddled with Claymore pellets. Had that bird been hit with the RPG he was aiming, close to a thousand gallons of flaming aviation fuel and helicopter pieces would have blown out all over our position.

Because I'd been out on listening post, I was one of the last to get a ration of water. Gut instinct told me I wouldn't get much and I was right. All I got was half a canteen. I knew it wouldn't last long. That morning, as I lifted the green plastic to my lips, I remembered all the old axioms about sipping and conserving the last bits of water. I slugged most of the bottle down and left a paltry few ounces as a token to my better judgment.

After first light, we began moving again. No time was taken for a breakfast of C rations. I don't think I had any food left, we'd left so much stuff behind at the beginning of our mission. Thirst and the need to get out of that place overwhelmed any sensations of hunger. If anybody ate, they ate on the run.

Sunlight crossed the treetops and slivers of light shot across the jungle floor. I felt better about being out of that clearing. The jungle offered cover and we used it to move swiftly among the trees. I'd lost all track of time by now. I'd been slogging along, one foot after the other, not really paying attention when a burst of automatic weapons fire brought me back to attention. As I lunged to the ground, the back of my neck prickled as the forest filled with the sound of machine guns, AK47s, and M16s. This time, the guys directly ahead of us were engaged in a firefight. The rest of us in the dirt tried to make as low a profile as possible. I craned my head to look but could see nothing through the foliage. Bullets whizzed over my head so I thought better of it and planted the side of my face in the dirt again. Through the din of the battle, I could hear a wounded man call for a medic. It seemed like only minutes passed before a medevac helicopter arrived. It landed away from the actual firefight and closer to my position. I watched three bullet holes appear on the side of it, just below the floor, as it lifted off.

I don't remember much after that. Thirst and heat slowly drained my energy and spirit. We wound our way through the jungle to the LZ we originally landed at. None of us cared about anything but getting out of there as we hungrily looked to the sky for the flight that would take us out of there. A sniper took occasional potshots at us and each crack of his weapon made us duck, but thankfully no one was hit. The third wave of helicopters was the one that lifted me out of there. I thought about the sniper till we were well out of his range. As we lifted away, my fear was cleansed with glorious altitude, wind, and light inside the helicopter. We landed near the firebase; now it was finally over.

Shoulders slumped, feet aching, and literally dying of thirst, I could barely walk from the helicopter. Ahead of me, to my delight and amazement, sat a water tank trailer. My first thought was that it might be empty or that it would get crowded before I got to it. I needed water desperately. One guy was just leaving it. He left it looking down as he screwed the cap back onto his canteen. I rushed to it, filled my canteen, and began drinking. I gulped down four full canteens of water, a gallon. My back rested against the tank as I sat there exhausted and panting

Scout Dog I befriended after offering it water.

while more arriving guys filled their canteens. My mind went blank as I fell into a wide-eyed dream state. I let it all go.

I saw our dog handler approaching from a distance with his scout dog: the dog that had almost attacked me before. I snapped out of my stupor and seized the opportunity to win him over. As he approached, head down, tongue out, and panting, I simply held my palm out and poured water onto it from my canteen. The handler knew what I was doing. He looked at me and simply dropped the leash. I sat motionless as the dog trotted up to me and began drinking out of my hand. When he was done drinking I petted him. He allowed me a few strokes before running back to his handler.

7

Women and Children

The effects of my bad drug experience are waning. I don't have the shakes anymore and I can look people in the eye. Nonetheless, I am just a lost, barely pubescent kid. Only barely past my twenty-first birthday, I am still stunned from my bad experience with drugs and I am too immature in too many areas to be a good soldier.

Vietnam was like a bad dream to me with dream sequences that went from bad to worse. Walking the fields and jungles of Vietnam, I watch men die or get dismembered. Little had changed in my human growth except for the training and conditioning the Army had given me. Though very much like an unfledged bird, I am now considered a grown man, and I carry a deadly weapon.

I'd gained some experience out here at the firebase. Now, the company lined up and prepared to fly back to the main base of Dau Tieng where we would work to contain and destroy the enemy in and around that city and its rubber plantation.

Anticipating, happy eyes looked upward at the formation of UH-1 helicopters coming in to take us back to our main base in Dau Tieng. Compared to where we'd been here at the fire support base, Dau Tieng was a vacation get-away with daily showers, tents, and a real mess hall. We would be operating out of there till we were thrown back into another one of the savage forward areas.

Dau Tieng sat nestled among the cooling trees of the Michelin rubber plantation. The ancient villages near it housed many peasant rubber workers, many of whom were Viet Cong sympathizers. The Michelin was also the first place I ever got shot at. I always felt that there was something queer about that. At home, we drove on Michelin tires.

Dau Tieng was considered a rear area and we had many of the comforts of home including a small PX, and even a pool. The entire base was encircled with multiple rows of coiled razor wire interspersed by fortified bunkers. Though any area could be hit at any time in Vietnam, a rear base camp was considered a safe place. The official designation of my unit was B Company, 2/12th Infantry (White Warriors), 25th Infantry Division. Though nearby Cu Chi was the headquarters of the 25th division, Dau Tieng was the headquarters of the 2/12th Inf.

Being in Dau Tieng finally gave us a chance to sleep properly and wear clean clothes. When a combat mission was announced, we'd put our gear on and simply walk out of the front gate or board two-and-a-half-ton trucks: sometimes to patrol, sometimes to set up ambush positions. Dau Tieng had its own runway which allowed large helicopter formations to pick us up and deliver us on complicated combat assaults. I hated all of it. Usually, by the time we found the enemy, they'd already seen us first. They'd shoot and disappear into the jungle. We killed many, many more of them than they did us, but it seemed we weren't really the ones in control. Most of the time they fired and ran. Sometimes they came in suicidal waves. They just didn't care about dying. Communist leadership commanded them and flawed ideals drove them. It was very clear to me that their war was about nothing more than taking by force and communism what others owned. The communists played by their own rules. Anything was fair to achieve their goals including starvation, torture, and mass murder.

Despite the comforts of Dau Tieng, we faced the realities of war, sometimes in a matter of minutes when we left the safety of the wire. I often felt certain a grenade would explode beside me or a bullet would tear through my chest. I'd have visions of myself bleeding in a childlike, fetal position with the enemy running up to me for the final kill as I lay there helpless. This fantasy Viet Cong had black, dead eyes and smelled of rancid sweat on threadbare, tattered, and unwashed cloth. Flashes of explosions and smoke always accompanied this unwanted phantasm. My ever-present bogeyman played havoc with me and my ability to continue being a soldier. I hated this duty. I had to get out of there somehow, some way before I was killed. Escaping my situation proved to be a slippery, convoluted road. The U.S. Army would not simply let me go. Even if they did I would have to live with myself as being a chicken and I couldn't do that. For now, however, I had to get out of here. I could almost feel death coming. In the end, I didn't have to worry about my pride. By the time my combat tours played themselves out, I'd seen more than my share of combat. I'd only succeeded in jumping from the frying pan into the fire. But at least I came out of the fire alive.

7. Women and Children

In Vietnam infantry rules were simple. Anyone in a free-fire zone, other than friendly troops, was not supposed to be there and was considered a target. We killed them before they could kill us. Things got tougher later as rules of engagement got forced on us, but for now, even unarmed people in free-fire zones were considered the enemy because they knew they shouldn't be there and they could be spies or enemy combatants. For undisciplined, inexperienced, or immature young men such as myself, split-second decisions could have disastrous consequences.

We walked out of the thicket, one day, where the jungle mixed with rubber trees near the edge of the Michelin Rubber Plantation. As far as I knew, we were in a free-fire zone. Plodding along mindlessly, there was usually no time to think or judge when things happened suddenly. My arm pushed aside thick, blocking foliage and there they were. Women and girls riding in a truck where I assumed one should not be. Even as I lifted my rifle to open fire on them, my conscience screamed at me not to but it was too late. My trained and programmed brain had already communicated to my brain, eyes, and arms. My forefinger followed and moved to the trigger. Its intentions were intentional yet not premeditated. At that moment, our medic knocked me to the ground with a tackling body blow.

That incident would stay with me. What, at the time, seemed like the right thing to do, would have destroyed so many lives, including my own. It still sits heavily in my thoughts. Had I shot up the people in that truck, I'd be dead now from alcohol or dope. There is no way I could have lived with it. I shudder as I write this. I almost did this ... but then, just several weeks later I watched death rain down on people only a few miles away. In some twisted cosmic joke, the same local people I thought had been spared from my careless trigger finger may have been killed for no reason by enemy rockets. After all, the majority of the people in the hamlets around Dau Tieng worked in the rubber plantation. They died right there in Dau Tieng on the edge of the plantation. It happened as we were leaving to patrol another area near the plantation.

It was relatively late in the day when we geared up and assembled for a large night patrol and ambush. For me, the worst part of infantry duty was leaving to go on a mission. Just when you thought you made it through another day, out you went again.

Our long column of helmeted, downward-gazing troops, slowly walked along the barbed-wire perimeter that was closest to the village of Dau Tieng or one of its hamlets. Golden light bathed us through the rubber trees. We trudged heavily along a ribbon of red dirt road that contrasted the vivid green plantation around it. The normal bustling sounds of the village muted as it settled down for the evening. A section of wire had been opened for us and we'd soon walk through it, past the town and into the jungle, where we'd arrive around sundown to stay overnight.

The familiar sound of incoming 122mm rockets came from behind us and we immediately dove for cover. Thankfully, a drainage ditch ran along both sides of the road to the left and right of us and we all had immediate, almost adequate protection. I thudded into the ditch on my right with a great feeling of relief. If I huddled low enough, the dirt enveloped me. Only seconds passed before the shock wore off and the screaming of the wounded began. I was immediately struck by its high pitch. These voices belonged to women and children in the village. The Viet Cong had probably missed their intended target or were retaliating against the villagers for collaborating with us. Many of them worked on our base and this could be their punishment.

As we climbed out of the drainage ditch and reoriented ourselves, more screaming voices joined those already wailing in pain. Other screams simply rose in intensity. I imagined muscles and tissue ripped from bone as I listened to the injured and dying. As I stood, I looked back and to the right 100 yards or so. Smoke from the exploded rockets and the subsequent fires they had ignited rose into the tropical afternoon. We dusted ourselves off. The company commander gave the order and we began walking again, leaving the devastation behind us.

Years later, while exiting the Veterans Assistance Office, during the enrollment phase at Queensborough Community College, in New York City, I was confronted by a pudgy, but cute girl who asked if I was a Vietnam veteran.

""Yes," I proudly answered.

"How many women and children did you kill?" she asked.

My long bout with drugs and alcohol had already begun and was picking up steam. On the way home from school I picked up a six-pack. When I got home I slowly drank it all. The warmth of the alcohol spread outwards from my belly to my brain and now allowed me the luxury of ignoring my emotions. I stared dumbly at the floor and a single tear turned into a torrent. I cried alone that night. I cried for the women and children at Dau Tieng and I cried for my 58,000+ dead brothers in

Workers in the Michelin Rubber Plantation.

Vietnam. I cried because my country had turned its back on me. I cried because the greatest effort of my life meant nothing.

Later in life, as an old man, my self-esteem and perspective of those events I witnessed as a kid would be tempered by maturity and steeled by historical facts. If I met that naive little hippie girl from the college again, I'd confront her with ferocity, logic, and tenacity. I'd quickly subjugate her intellectually and instill into her whatever facts I could about the untold millions dead in Vietnam, Cambodia, and Laos caused by our failure in that war. I'd be sure to leave her feeling at least as bad as she did me ... and for her to experience some of the pain I and others like me would feel for most if not all of our lives.

8

Strange Grenades and Tarot Cards

Under a canopy of rubber trees, lying on a cot in the green canvas cave that is my tent, I am asleep swaddled in a camouflaged poncho liner. It is soft, fluffy, and comfortable, the favorite army-issued piece of equipment we have here. My cot is the third one back on the right.

I dream of Greenwich Village. Ellen is in love with me and is attempting to take my virginity. Everything about her is soft. Her eyes, her skin, even her pubic hair is soft ... but I am not ready. I kiss her neck and my fingers move over her velvet skin. I go through the motions quite well but I am too nervous. Jeff and Dee are in the bed next to us making out, but I know their interest lies in what will happen next between Ellen and me.

Excited voices outside my tent rouse me. I awaken curious but unafraid. Despite its proximity to hell, Vietnam was an easy place to wake up in if the waking was done in a rear area.

"Third platoon has a body count and brought back some VC's stuff."

The voice comes clear through my open tent as I swing my legs over the side of my cot to put my boots on. As I hurry I strain to listen.

Sunlight blasts me when I exit the gloom of the tent. My arm rests on the unfolded tent-flap of the entry as I look to see what direction the voices came from. Off to my left, several guys are standing clustered around a lump on the ground. Squinting, I can see it is a soldier's equipment. The shoulder harness with attached waist belt is obvious and my curiosity grows as I start walking towards it. I speed up. One of the guys is gingerly opening up the pack and spreading the items inside on the ground. My curiosity rises. I want to see the gear and weaponry.

I am ten feet away and I can clearly see the grenade. My legs slow my approach without conscious thought and all my senses are alerted.

This is a Viet Cong's equipment. The grenade attached to the harness is homemade. It has been manufactured out of a soda can. There is a threaded detonator screwed into the top of it.

I join the others standing around the web gear and I realize we are all alternately looking down on the gear and each other. Few of us bend over to touch it. Then it dawns on me that having this here could be trouble. I have no idea who brought it here and I wonder if anybody in charge even knows about it. Enemy equipment was very often booby-trapped. My instincts tell me nobody has inspected these items before bringing them back to our base camp and this only increases my curiosity.

As if reading my thoughts, two of the guys turn and leave. I sense they want no part of the possible danger or trouble we could get into. Without looking at the guy still standing beside me, I risk it all and bend over to pick up the entire harness, leaving the backpack and other stuff on the ground. After all, somebody brought it here. I'm sure they jangled it around more than I will standing here. Holding it all by the suspender straps, I slowly turn the gear in the air in front of me. There is the grenade, an empty water canteen, and a folded plastic pouch. Carefully, I lower it all back to the ground and begin inspecting it again. With a careful finger, I prod and poke till I talk myself into believing I can safely go further.

Now my attention turns to the most important item, the grenade. It is attached to the waist belt very simply. If I'm going to do this, I have to safely remove it, inspect it and make sure it can't explode. Though I know I'm one of the least qualified in the entire company to be doing this, I'm sure this is probably how it's done. I do it by the numbers: visually and cautiously. This grenade has been on the belt for a long time. It is attached with a very simple clip. The soda can paint and enamel has worn in spots and there are small dents all over it. The seams on the metal are intact and the detonator has been in place since its manufacture. It is sealed in place with some kind of wax or plastic. My overall impression is that it has not been tampered with and that it is in fact only a dead soldier's equipment.

Holding my breath, I grab the grenade while holding the belt on the ground with my boot and give it a good tug. It comes off the belt easily.

Normally, explosive material is surprisingly heavy. Unlike gunpowder, it is usually poured into grenades or artillery as a molten liquid that then solidifies into a plaster-like material. This grenade was surprisingly light. Between the aluminum can casing, the explosive content, and the detonator, it barely weighed a pound. Something was not right here. I kept turning the grenade in my hand, shaking it gently, and looking at it from all angles.

"I'm going to unscrew the detonator and see what's in this mother fucker." I turned and grinned at the guy still with me.

"Yeah?" He stepped back about four feet and I had to smile; forty feet would not have been enough if he really thought it might explode.

With my thumb and forefinger, I tightly clasped the body of the detonator. It consisted of an aluminum body with a pull pin. It was probably American-made. Carefully, I turned it counter-clockwise. The seal broke relatively easily. After that, I did half a turn at a time. I figured I was at the most dangerous part. If this thing was booby-trapped, it was in the detonator. When the entire mechanism was loose I gingerly lifted it out of the grenade with my thumb and forefinger and to my surprise, there was nothing after the threads: there was no blasting cap. This was a fake grenade. I looked inside of it and saw green.

The entire grenade body was filled with marijuana. This must have been his bank stash. I figured that he had been holding on to it to sell it. I thought about the possibility of him having sold to one of us, had he lived.

I screwed the top back into the grenade and turned my attention to the pouch on the shoulder part of the harness. The pouch was a simple affair. A simple piece of folded plastic, it was tied in a shoelace style with simple twine. Holding it closed with one finger, I undid the lacing. Then, I unfolded the flaps carefully with a finger. Inside was a crude binder. This was his personal stuff.

Inside were two items. One was some sort of ID card. The other was a black and white photo of his family clad in traditional Vietnamese garb: three people: a man, a woman, and a child who would never see him again. My bravado changed and settled. It was now a weight, albeit a small one, still a weight. It was too light to feel at the time but it was added to the others that I would carry in my life because I would never forget that photograph. For now, I had to stifle distracting sentiments. They were dangerous.

I don't miss home as much as some of the guys. If I walk quietly and look carefully from the corner of my eyes, I can see guys retreated to personal spaces where they contemplate family or girlfriends back in the states. I know exactly how they feel even though there is little for me back home. My good times are long gone. If I'd been ripped from the best times of my life, I'd miss home too. Though I feel resentful for having been hijacked into this situation by the draft board of a country that doesn't care, and though I constantly fear the danger, being in the Army has given me back my health, some self-confidence, and a sense of belonging. There is loneliness to be sure, but these days are so much better than those bleak and gray waning days of the winter after my bad experience with LSD ... and having to live with my mother.

There were others like me, not totally unhappy to be here. Some had been in jail. Some never had a home or two nickels to rub together. More than once I watched with perplexed amusement as some formerly impoverished city boy delighted in eating the same C rations others would forgo. The guys who had the most back home had the most to lose. Their minds were always elsewhere.

I don't know where I picked up the Tarot cards. It might've been in Greenwich Village while on leave or Haight-Ashbury in San Francisco when I visited there on a weekend during infantry training at Fort Ord. Colorful and mysterious, they sparked my imagination when I took them out of the box to look at them. I bought them for under two dollars. They were supposed to be for fun: just a curiosity.

Another one of the comforts of home at Dau Tieng, besides the tent and cot, was personal possessions. One could feel a sense of connection, sentiment, and a little humanity among the letters, magazines, and souvenirs at the bottom of footlockers and duffel bags.

I found myself rummaging around my own stuff one day and found the Tarot cards I had forgotten about.

As I spread them out on my footlocker to reveal their mystical images, I remembered why I bought them. Every card had pictures of ancient, interesting characters whose depictions appeared to have been rendered centuries ago. I spent time going through the cards one by one. I understood nothing of the meaning of the persons portrayed or how the deck worked. Shuffling the cards and flipping them over one by one, it was easy to develop a storyline from the pictures. If I used my imagination, I could probably have some fun doing a reading for someone.

"Grzesik, whatcha got there?" One of the guys had come into my tent and was looking over my shoulder.

"Tarot cards; I can read the future." I grinned up at him

"Oh yeah? You want to tell me my future?" He sounded sarcastic but interested at the same time. His eyes looked serious.

That was the way it started. I shuffled the deck and began flipping cards. The first one was the Ten of Wands. It depicted an individual struggling with ten sticks. This was so easy. "You will be trying to hold together and move many things," I said

The next card was the King of Swords. It depicted a king on a throne with a sword. "You will face a powerful leader with a weapon." I looked up at him soberly.

The following card was the Nine of Pentacles. It portrayed a woman surrounded by lush foliage with a bird on her shoulder. "A woman in a garden awaits you," I ad-libbed mysteriously.

The fourth card was the Three of Cups. It showed three joyous women holding chalices of drink high in the air. "Joyous women will celebrate you with drinks held high." I laughed and smiled.

"No shit? Tell me more," he said with eager eyes.

It caught on quickly with the guys. By the time I did two or three more readings for them, I had it worked out to only drawing ten cards. Soon it dawned on me that my comrades were taking these sessions too seriously. I could tell by their intent expressions and furrowed brows when I did the readings. I put the thought to the back of my mind and continued doing them because they wanted me to. Then one day, in the middle of "reading" the cards, I heard voices outside my tent. I went to investigate. Three men stood there in line, sweating in the sun with serious looks on their faces, waiting to have their cards read. Gloom and panic fell over me. In one moment all the bad possibilities and ramifications of continuing this hit me. I told the guys to leave because I had business to tend to, and I disposed of the cards by ripping them to shreds and dumping them in a distant trash can. It took the rest of the day to shake off the uncomfortable feeling I had.

9

Five Crazy Days in Dau Tieng

They are like a dream. Long ago and far away. Those balmy nights still linger in my memory. Perfumed night air that invited me out of my tent still lends a whisper of its bouquet. I always thought Vietnam had the faintest pleasant aroma.

I'd go outside into the night not to escape the tent's confines, but to breathe in the essence that was Vietnam during peaceful respites. Even the tent canvas waxed fragrant with a must that was more soothing than offensive. I piece the memories together carefully, like shards of a broken mirror I never bothered looking into. I do it carefully so as not to cut myself on their sharp edges. If I leave the bad, the rest is so sweet. You've never lived, till you've almost died.

Those tropical nights settled on Dau Tieng serenely but powerfully. Voices mellowed to whispers and even mundane jobs like guard duty drew little complaint from the company guys. These were nights to relax, joke, and chat. Some men would have a beer, others would smoke a joint. I envied the guys who could partake in these revelries. Because of the bad effects booze and pot had on me now, I abstained from those merriments. I'd watch and listen with fond amusement as their raucous laughter lifted into the sky like the sound of bells. Only the blare of the rising sun could lift the magic off Dau Tieng.

I stood in my tent, pulling down the brim of my jungle hat, about to step out into the midday blaze. With the new day came oppressive heat. It settled on us like a weight. We wore jungle hats in the rear base camps with brims stretched, molded, and folded into individual style statements that were also utilitarian. One had to have shade in Vietnam. The jungle hat rated as one of the favorite pieces of Army-issued equipment. Everyone took great pains to wear it with individuality.

Outside my tent with an M-60 Machine Gun.

The always smiling George suddenly appeared at the entrance to the tent. Framed by the sunlight in the back of him, he beamed at me.

"Hey, Grzesik, whatcha doin'?"

"Hey, Jungle George, nuthin ... maybe goin' to the PX." I smiled at him. One had to smile with George.

"Hey, let's go to the pool."

"Sure but I ain't got a bathing suit."

"Don't worry, I'll get you one."

I'd heard about the pool. It had served the French overseeing the plantation during its heyday. The plantation itself stretched 31,000 acres and we patrolled it regularly as did the enemy. George reappeared with swim trunks in hand and we walked, threading our way between the rubber trees, to the pool. Once there, we changed and got into the line of three or four guys waiting their turn to check their clothes at the clothing hut. Then came my turn.

"I take clothes and give you number." Smiling at me, through a window in the property check shack, was the most beautiful Vietnamese girl I had ever seen.

"C'mon man, hurry up," somebody chided me from the line to my rear.

I'd been caught off guard by her perfect white teeth and raven black hair. Her glowing skin bore no lines of worry or war. She had the innocence of youth and the easygoing grace of the privileged class. I checked my clothes, slipped the numbered receipt tag around my wrist, and began my doomed friendship with Sandy.

I remembered the words of the instructor at the In-Country Orientation Class, "You don't need to try to get involved with any women while you're here. It ain't gonna happen and it will be nothing but trouble for you. You need to be thinking about your job, and how to stay alive while you're here so you don't go home in a body bag."

I'd just turned twenty-one two months earlier. Behind my youthful, hungry eyes lay an arrogance and innocence that was outmatched only by my inexperience and lack of finesse. I said many boastful things to this exquisite young woman and with the art of a genteel oriental belle, she listened to them with graceful acquiescence. She bore none of the traits of the modern women in America. She became enamored with me not by what I was saying but by my eagerness to impress her. It took two days for us to be infatuated with each other.

I plied her with compliments. I fed her stories of my daring and courage. I described the United States. I said what I thought I had to, to curry favor with her. Then, after only knowing her for a few days, on a stupid impulse, I decided to impress her by pulling a practical joke on her. The puerile idiot in me came out and overrode what little common sense I had. Somewhere near the pool, I found a dead rat. I thought it would be funny to hear her scream in mock horror. I placed it on her counter at the check-in window. Unfortunately, her horror was real. Sandy left that day and never came back again. Though I went to the pool several more times I never saw her again. It took a while for it to dawn on me that I was most likely the reason she left. A dead rat left that way symbolized a threat almost everywhere. It certainly did where I came from. For years I winced at that memory.

It might have been Sandy I was thinking about the day I decided to walk across the runway at Dau Tieng, on my way to our modest commissary. The shortest distance there was across the runway. To walk around it probably added a mile in distance. I stood at the edge of the strip and I stared at it. Stateside, in a peace-time army, doing this would be a major transgression punishable by at least an Article 15. I knew that it probably wouldn't be looked upon favorably here either, but I took the chance. Thoughtless with caution to the wind, I casually began strolling towards the runway. I'd gotten very used to watching where I walked and I did so now. Between me and the actual landing strip lay a stretch of raggedy, ankle-high grass so I kept my eyes down and watched

Sandy.

where I walked. Halfway to the runway, I spotted the tail remnant of an exploded Chinese mortar. My eyes combed over it carefully and I walked a small circle around it before touching it to make sure it wasn't booby-trapped or only partially exploded. My fingers picked deftly at the edges of it before picking it up. I felt quite pleased with myself. This was going to be a great war souvenir.

My eyes were still glued to my prize as I approached the edge of the runway. I took a couple of more steps when suddenly everything felt wrong. My senses told me something was amiss. I whirled to the left and right before I saw the air traffic control tower. Inside it, two men waved their arms at me wildly. Luckily, my reflexes engaged in only a fraction of a second and I bolted across the runway. As I ran I instinctively looked to the right. There was a propeller plane bearing down on me. It got larger with every frame of my reference. Two more steps and it was almost on top of me. I'd almost made it to the other side when it zoomed by the spot I had just been in. I made it across the runway but I kept running. I kept running even after I left the flight area. Situations like this could get serious fast and I didn't need any more trouble with officers or NCOs.

Spotter plane landing on the Dau Tieng runway.

We Had to Get Out of That Place

As I ran it dawned on me, I'd almost gotten killed in Vietnam by a plane. It would have been a strange way to die, but many things about this war were strange. I took runway photos later.

A cloak of rubber trees closed around me once I ran clear of the flight line. I slowed my run to a trot. My pace slowed again when I felt I had created enough distance between me and the air traffic control tower. Not wanting to arouse suspicion, I eventually slowed to a walk when I found myself in an area of wooden plank buildings. They looked more permanent than the tents of my company area. A light chain snaked away from one of these buildings. It made clinking sounds. I took a closer look. At the end of it, a dog was cavorting with a monkey. I stared, incredulous. Both animals weighed about eight pounds and they rolled round and round on the ground in an ecstasy of abandon and playfulness. Astounded at what I was seeing, I stood and watched.

"That's Claymore and RPG." I looked to my left. A sergeant E-6 stood pointing towards the animals from the doorway of one of the hooches.

"They always play like that?" I asked.

"All the time," he replied. "Wow," I said as he went back inside.

I approached carefully and presented my hand to both animals, eventually summoning the courage to pet the monkey. Finally, I picked it up. Its little paws grabbed all my buttons and my shirt. Bright eyes twinkled at me and white teeth flashed. A warm feeling spread through me. Then, the little fellow jumped out of my arms onto the rubber tree next to me. He climbed halfway up and jumped down onto the roof of the building. I had to smile. The experience made me feel more human, as if I was home playing with my dog. I enticed the monkey off the roof and he jumped into my waiting arms. I swung him back and forth and flung him up into the tree. He climbed up again and jumped back onto the roof. We went round and round that way. I don't know who tired first or who enjoyed it more and I never made it to the commissary.

By the time I returned to the B Company area, guys were suiting up to go on patrol. I barely made it back in time. I was glad we were heading out. My eyes darted furtively, looking to see if an officer from the aviation unit had followed or found me. I imagined his words as I examined my gear and made last-minute preparations for going out. "One of your guys crossed the runway and almost got hit by a plane." He never came.

With a snap of my wrist, I flipped open my rucksack and eyed the contents. Satisfied that I wasn't forgetting anything I scanned the grenades and other items on my web gear and swung it over my shoulder and onto my back. As I struggled with the brass buckle on the front of my pistol belt, I heard my sergeant's voice as he walked by our tents. "C'mon people, hurry it up." Low grunts and complaints followed.

"Same shit, different day" someone proclaimed. "Just stop your bitchin and get ready," he snapped back.

Though I'm sure the actual travel time to the jungle was a lot longer, it always seemed like it was just minutes. That dreaded walk or truck ride was the only safe time we had, after that, I was on a combat mission again. Somewhere outside of Dau Tieng, in the late afternoon, I found myself walking again.

I'd been in-country less than a month and I was getting a distinct impression that the way some guys stayed safe here was by putting new guys between themselves and danger. It seemed I was always on listening post, walking point, or something similarly dangerous even though I didn't really know what I was doing yet. Today I was walking flank. I'd be on the side of the company with another guy while we moved. Perhaps I felt sorry for myself as a private, but years later, when I had grown to be an experienced soldier, I still felt I had been put in danger too often for a new guy.

We walked out of the rubber plantation into scrub and then jungle. I cocked my head to the right and down as I lifted a branch with my left forearm and pushed it out of my way. One of the problems with walking flank was that nobody walked ahead of you or behind you. It was just the two of you. Vegetation had not been shoved aside or flattened by other feet yet.

Blinking sweat out of my eyes, I scanned the jungle for moving helmets off to my right. Worry gnaws at me. I don't want to lose sight of these guys and, how the hell am I supposed to do that and fight my way through this jungle at the same time? I'm making so much damn noise, but I have to keep up with the company.

One hundred meters later we punched through another thick section of jungle and when we came out of it on the other side the main element was gone; the company was nowhere to be seen. We froze in place and listened, straining to hear some faint sound of receding steps in the forest but we heard nothing. In one second we'd walked out of the safety of our infantry formation and into a hostile jungle in enemy territory. We were lost.

There was nothing to do but walk. I thought about sitting and waiting for help but dismissed the idea because it felt too rooted in helplessness and vulnerability. The guy with me didn't offer any helpful input. I took a minute to figure the most probable direction the column had been going and we headed that way.

Every tree, every branch, and every feature in that jungle took on new importance as we walked. It felt like I had to try to memorize every small detail in the green labyrinth or get swallowed further by it. A gnawing tension and panic began setting in. Pressure built behind my eyes as sweat rolled down my face. We picked up the pace because dusk was approaching. It would be getting dark in an hour or so.

We'd walked less than half a mile when I saw him. There, about a hundred feet in front of me stood an American soldier. Before I even had time to process my thoughts, he whirled pointing his M16 rifle at us. We'd walked up on one of our other platoons. "Who are you? What the fuck are you doing? I almost shot you," he said.

We both stammered. We were at a total loss for words. There was nothing to be said. We screwed up and got lost. Our platoon was contacted by radio and two guys were sent back to get us.

Though we both felt a bit sheepish, relief washed over us. None of this seemed to be a big deal to anybody else. I got the impression that this had happened before ... and why wouldn't it? The jungle could be black as night in the middle of the day. Sometimes visibility was only as far as one could reach, other times, wide green vistas opened up when they were least expected.

The path of least resistance back to our platoon was actually a path. Animals or perhaps people had worn a faint trail on the forest floor and we followed that.

The four of us were halfway back to our platoon when I heard it. Immediately on my left, not more than six feet away from me, bush rustled and I heard the pounding of feet running away from where I stood. I turned to my left and pointed my rifle, then I immediately ran forward to my guys and grabbed one by the shoulder. They were still walking. Apparently, they had heard nothing.

"Hey man, did you hear that? There was someone right next to me and he ran away," I said excitedly.

They looked at me like I was nuts. One of the guys who had been sent back to get us did not want to be bothered with this. He down-played it. I immediately understood. There were enough bad guys in the forest without going looking for them. All three of them blew my concerns off. I wasn't crazy, I knew what I had heard. The fact that this guy could have killed me made this even more important. If it hadn't been for the fact that he panicked and ran, I could be dead, and the guys with me could be dead too.

I was still talking about it when we arrived back at the platoon site. I told my platoon sergeant and he also disregarded me. At this point, I was getting angry and frustrated so I strode briskly towards the lieutenant's area to try to tell him.

Someone near the lieutenant looked up and said, "Don't bother the lieutenant now, can't you see he's busy?" I burst out telling anyone who would listen what had happened. I got assertive like I never had been before. My face flushed red, as I walked closer to the lieutenant as he squatted with others around a map on the ground. They all looked up at me. "Sir, there is someone out there. He was right next to me."

The lieutenant looked up, his eyes wide. It was the kind of look you get when you tell people that the reason you're late is that you were in a car accident. I was finally allowed to tell my story in its entirety and I was taken very seriously.

Within five minutes of my telling the lieutenant the story, he got on a radio and called in artillery fire. In the morning a small element was sent out to recon the impact area. They found blood trails. That guy could have killed me but instead, I might have killed him.

It had been a crazy five days but it wasn't over yet. Walking out of there I stumbled and almost twisted my ankle. I tried to correct, but with a weighty pack on my back, all I succeeded in doing was falling awkwardly. Somehow my lower right leg lodged behind my left leg as I fell. The left leg closed like a nutcracker around the lower right leg.

I could barely walk. I limped back to wherever we were going and in a short time, I could hardly walk at all. The next morning I went on sick call. After a very thorough examination, the doctor could find nothing, not even the smallest scratch or black-and-blue mark. He accused me of malingering and made an appointment for me to see a specialist. He warned me that if there was no positive result for an injury, he would write me up for malingering. I felt shame.

I don't remember where I wound up. I think it might have been at the battalion headquarters. Apprehension wracked me. Malingering was a serious charge and an accusation the other guys would not take lightly. To my surprise, I was greeted by a cheerful doctor. He read my file briefly and said, "Tell me about your leg."

I described my fall in detail and blurted out that nobody believed me. He looked at me pensively, reached into a drawer, and pulled out a measuring tape. He then measured both legs to compare them. "Your left leg is significantly swollen. I'm giving you two days of light duty."

The entire appointment had taken less than ten minutes. I pulled guard duty for the next two days. By the third day, the pain was almost gone and I went on combat patrol again.

As usual, we walk in simmering heat waiting to be shot at. We're plodding this time, eyes down, single file, outside of some hamlet near the edge of the jungle by Dau Tieng. Nobody wants to be here.

A loud explosion shatters the silence. The sound crashes through our ranks and everyone drops to their bellies. I'm shaken by the blast and I wonder if anyone's hit. I'm not. A row of heads on prone bodies swivels in all directions as everyone wonders the same thing.

"Medic!" The scream comes from my front in the area of the explosion. High pitched and panicked, the voice is child-like. It reminds me of terrible injuries from childhood: the scream of a child having a car door slammed on their hand or a kid breaking a limb on the playground. I imagine a fetal position.

I crane my head harder for a look. Only my head and chest are raised; my body is in a half pushup position. Behind me, someone is coming fast. My head turns as I hear the thud of running feet. Just as I turn, our medic comes into view. He is running head down and stooped low. His bag is in his hand and he looks scared. For a second our eyes lock and he slows down. He thought it was me, but no. He keeps running. My back and shoulders ache from the arch of pushing my head up so I settle back down into the vegetation around me. All is silent but for footsteps. Is this a prelude to the main attack? People trot by me towards the wounded man and I hear muted voices ahead. Finally, after ten minutes or so, they carry him out on a makeshift litter. As they pass me I can see the bandage. It is wrapped around his entire leg. I can see stains all over it. It looks like a murky liquid is rising from the wound, but it is not the color of blood. It is almost clear. The guy being carried away has a stunned look about him and he makes no sound.

Later after it was all over, and the last droning beats of the medevac helicopter fade into the horizon the medic walks up to me. "He wasn't paying attention and tripped the wire on a booby-trapped grenade. When I saw you on the ground, I thought it was you."

I simply stared at him. It could have easily been me.

10

Boom-boom

"Hey, GI, you want boom-boom?"

From the poorest hamlets to the blaring bars of Saigon, women sold themselves to American soldiers. Our young faces and toned bodies lent newness to their ancient profession. These girls really liked us. Besides being young, muscular, and disease-free, we had lots of money and big, sincere smiles. We considered these Oriental women extraordinarily beautiful and sensual. They, in turn, often thought the same of us. Some enjoyed their job. Many young men lost their virginity in Vietnam. I was one of them.

On one occasion, when I allowed myself the delight of one of these young women I was startled to have her shudder beneath me uncontrollably. At first, I didn't know what was happening, but then I realized she was having a powerful orgasm. I still remember fleeting, ridiculous notions of getting her out of that place: the place she probably wanted to leave anyway and making her mine. She was in her early teens with looks that immediately pulled at the heartstrings. I was twenty-one and barely past virginity. There was no mistaking the longing and shame in her eyes when I left as our eyes locked briefly. I'd have felt better about myself if she had been more detached and emotionless because I felt the connection between us. I believe she did also. I walked away knowing we were both wasting our precious youth.

Occasionally, prostitutes found their way to our bunkers. In Vietnam, bunker guard duty was considered an easy duty by foot soldiers. The only better scenario was to have no duty at all and sleep on a cot in one's tent. It happened only occasionally. Many infantry units rarely saw their base camps. We were lucky in that regard. Fortified fighting positions dotted the perimeter behind the coiled barbed wire that encircled Dau Tieng. The sandbagged bunkers protected us from bullets and shrapnel, but we didn't really like being in those musty, confined enclosures because insects scurried back and forth across the floors, spider webs hung in the corners, and sometimes there were snakes. Bunkers needed visual inspection before entering. Ours had cots and large slits allowing for limited vision out, and a place to return fire in case of attack. For the most part, we lounged outside, with our rifles, in the tropical air. Here we had a better view of the area outside the wire. Sometimes, some of the savvier guys snuck girls in through the wire. They'd frolic the night away and sneak them back out before dawn.

One morning our Company Commander called a formation. During a surprise inspection, one of these girls had been caught in a bunker. She was searched and found with a sketch of the perimeter. She'd been making drawings of the base for the Viet Cong. I'm sure she was tortured and killed by the South Vietnamese interrogators she was handed over to.

This war spared no one and there was no end to its cruelty, not even to children. We walked out of Dau Tieng on another operation one evening. As usual, we were setting up a night ambush or blocking force. Simply put, we'd sit there all night, taking turns catnapping and waiting for someone to walk into our field of fire.

We were just setting up when I heard a commotion and voices off

Bunker guard duty on the Dau Tieng perimeter.

to my right in thick foliage. I walked over to investigate and saw one soldier struggling to get his gear off. Another stood looking down. On the ground, a half-naked soldier rhythmically thrust his pelvis up and down. He was having sex with a prostitute. Thinking about it, I imagined the usual peasant whore found around the villages. They were never as good-looking as the professional prostitutes. When I looked closely I was stunned to see a naked post-pubescent child. Horror welled up in me and I sprang forward to stop him. Before I could get anywhere, I was gently tackled by a guy I hadn't seen. Pity and sarcasm tinged his voice as he quietly informed me that babysan was charging five dollars per man and that she was well worth it. Gazing at her from the corner of my vision and trying not to make eye contact, I realized they were right. She was beautiful. I stood there flushed and confused. I walked away and left behind another part of my innocence.

Two or three days later, we again went out on an operation near the base. This time the distance was greater and we went by truck. We drove through Dau Tieng or some village near it. Along the way, we passed that same girl on a bicycle going the other way. I yelled to her and waved from the back of the deuce-and-a-half truck. I smiled and expected the same smile in return. After all, I was her would-be hero.

Her eyes flashed hatred and contempt. She gave me the finger and I turned away feeling shame, anger, and bewilderment.

11

New Guys

New guys in Vietnam usually got the worst jobs, and too often were placed in danger until they were in favor or proved themselves valuable. I considered this usury cowardly and inept leadership. I knew seven men who got killed in their first weeks in Vietnam. My friend from New York, Ricky, did, as did six men I came into my division with.

Some new guys simply stopped acknowledging authority. They stopped taking any orders they didn't like. They knew no one had their interests at heart. I certainly wasn't going to be in favor any time soon, so I also slowly but surely stopped allowing myself to be used. It was a liberating but simultaneously perilous posture to take. I feared reprisals.

The TET offensive of 1968 was over. We had beaten back the Viet Cong and NVA inflicting incredible, devastating losses on them, yet the discipline and morale of American units was slipping. Few people back in the world supported us and many of us were beginning to wonder why we were fighting. I began to believe that the old-timers did not want to take risks so they sent new guys out into the most dangerous jobs. Besides suspecting it was a pretty good way to keep themselves safe, I figured they did not want to lose the combat-hardened guys they relied on when the chips were down. We were being used as cannon fodder.

There was a learning process for new guys and the guys taking advantage of them. The new guy realizes one day that when he stops being blindly obedient for a minute, the user hesitates. He thinks, "The new guy is getting wise." He fears this because a defiant soldier is problematic in war. The user, usually higher ranking, may be blamed for that soldier's behavior or he might be exposed for his lack of leadership. Also, he has to start treating that person more fairly or he may get no more compliance from him.

I'd been given the dangerous positions of walking point or flank so many times, I figured nothing I could do could get me in more danger than my sergeants and officers were already putting me in. I was tired of it and knew I had to make a stand. One day, while walking point, I walked up on a water buffalo. I stopped, paralyzed with fear. I'd heard about these animals. They could kill you and they would kill you if provoked. They were considered semi-domesticated. I froze even more as it began pawing the ground with an angry hoof. My thoughts whirled. I mulled over every option I had. There was nothing I could do to protect myself but fire a full magazine into the beast.

"What's the hold-up?" The voice came through the radio clipped to my helmet.

"There's a water buffalo in front of me about to charge me."

"The captain says keep moving."

"Like hell I will" I whispered under my breath.

Now the animal was about to charge me. Flicking the selector switch to fully automatic, I raised my M16 rifle and prepared to fire. I planned to put a burst of twenty bullets into the creature's head and face. I didn't give a damn. I knew one bullet wouldn't stop it, only anger it. At that moment, the little three and a half foot tall boy who had been minding the beast started whipping the animal with a switch. The kid's shrill voice sounded panicked. He whipped the water buffalo with a frenzy as if he knew I was about to kill it. I looked at the spectacle before me and thought for a second that the animal might attack the kid. It jumped sideways. The kid continued whipping it, but on the rump now, as they both moved away. The transmissions ordering me to move continued over the radio. I ignored them till I knew there was a safe distance between me and that behemoth. I was about to move when someone from the rear walked up to me and said, "The captain wants to know what's going on and what's the holdup."

"There was a fuckin' water buffalo, man. I ain't walking into no fuckin' water buffalo."

He relieved me and I walked back into the column a little smarter than I was before. My understanding of these dynamics continued back at basecamp after we got back to Dau Tieng later that day. I was in the process of arranging my gear down by my bunk when I heard a commotion outside my tent. I went to investigate. Several tents down, a crowd was forming. I trotted over to see what was up. Inside a gathering circle of men stood our machine gunner and his ammo bearer. They both faced each other in the middle of the impromptu arena with the M60 machine gun balanced between them on its tripod and the end of its barrel. An altercation was about to kick off about whether the ammo bearer had to clean the machine gun. I ran back to my tent and grabbed my camera.

At one point I had been given the role of ammo bearer. My skinny, 140-pound frame could not handle the extra 37 pounds of weight. I already struggled under the weight of the other gear I had to carry in the jungle. After collapsing twice, I was relieved and the weight was given to another new guy: the good-natured and affable Midwestern guy I was looking at now. He was a corn-fed country boy about six foot two and at least 250 pounds. As I watched and listened, it became apparent to me that he questioned the gunner's order to clean the machine gun. He reasoned that he was already carrying ammo that wasn't even his and he'd be damned if he would clean the machine gun. I reveled in his rebellion.

Machine gunner and ammo bearer facing off regarding who should clean the weapon.

To me, this was just another example of a naïve new guy coming of age. I watched with delight as the gunner backed away, his eyes lowered, knowing he could not win this fight. The ammo bearer outweighed him by at least 70 pounds.

Things continued this way. Too often I found myself walking ahead of the unit on point, or on the side of it: walking flank. I had no choice but to keep walking these deadly positions. Positions were assigned and I had to obey orders. On most days I was dealt bad hands and I felt that they were dealt from the bottom of the deck.

A couple of new guys showed up in the unit while we were out on an operation. I eyed them balefully. Their new dark green fatigues and pink skin shone like a beacon. Their sparkling fresh eyes gleamed eager to please. They were nothing more than fresh meat for the butcher block. I knew what they were in for and I avoided them. Any communication with them was hesitant and halting. I realized that part of me discerned them as pariahs. I had enough troubles; I didn't need theirs. Was I becoming jaded? Could I become an exploitative bastard like many of these older guys? I could not see lasting in this insanity an entire year. I had to get out of there.

"Grzesik, take these two guys with you and set up a listening post. Set up fifty meters forward of our position." The lieutenant pointed a direction.

My shoulders slumped. I was still a new guy for all intents and purposes and I didn't know what I was doing yet. The men I had just been put in charge of were brand new. I'd never seen them before. The absurdity of it all and the hopelessness converged into a knot in my stomach. Morose and resentful, I plodded out with the two of them, trying not to look as unsure of myself as I felt. I strode long-legged. My mind was racing and didn't want my thoughts interrupted. The new guys kept asking me questions so I told them to shut up and follow me. We walked a straight line out into the bush in the direction the lieutenant had pointed. The forest wasn't too thick and the walking was easy. I did my best to memorize the route we took. After about fifty yards, we came upon a 10 × 10–foot clearing. "We're gonna set up here," I said to them in a whisper.

The jungle thickened ahead and I didn't want to walk any farther away anyway. We got down. I squatted into a cross-legged sitting position to begin taking stock of our situation. It took me less than ten seconds to realize I'd forgotten to bring a radio. My face flushed. I felt rage and shame. I thought it over and decided to go back by myself to get one. I told the new guys to stay put: that I'd be back in a few minutes. Caution to the wind, I practically ran back. Darkness was falling and I had newbies out there without a compass or radio. I figured my platoon would know who I was. After all, I'd left there just a little while ago. Everybody was still where I'd left them when I arrived. They all looked at me stupidly and I realized that if I had been a Vietcong, I could have shot the lot of them.

"I forgot to bring a radio," I stammered with simultaneous shame and anger. All I got was dumbfounded looks from everyone ... except the lieutenant. "Will somebody please go with this man?" He said it softly, in an angry voice.

The word "please" was not spoken with any civility. It was hissed in frustration and he would not look at me. A sergeant from Brooklyn accompanied me back. He was a street-wise, tough guy who had a lot of combat experience. The four of us set up for the night and we took turns on guard while the others catnapped.

Around three in the morning, I heard the first movement. It sounded like a slither. Then it happened again. The sound came closer. Now it was a slither and a rustle. The sounds came even closer. I woke everyone who was asleep. As we began preparing ourselves for the worst, every movement we made sounded ten times louder to us than it really was. My heart pounded in my chest so loudly that I thought the others and whoever was out there might hear it. They couldn't, of course. I slowly leaned over towards the sergeant. "We should call in artillery," I whispered.

"By the time we did, we'd give our position away, and besides, we're too close. Sit tight for now," he replied.

The thought of sitting and doing nothing but waiting unsettled me even more. The sounds were now about twenty feet ahead of us when I heard a loud snort, a scream, and just afterward, the thudding sound of multiple sets of hooves running. Wild pigs had walked up to us and panicked when they smelled us.

Wild pigs had just caused the greatest terror I'd experienced since coming to Vietnam.

12

Escape

I was still very new to the unit when I almost got wounded by an RPG. It happened during a long, running battle in the jungle (see War Dog Twice, chapter 6). Only the luck of the draw prevented me from catching a piece of shrapnel from the RPG that exploded twenty feet away from me. I stood swaying, staggering, and struggling to keep my balance from the push of the explosion when I first saw his malevolent eyes on me.

"Maybe now you'll pay attention." He had said with hatred and disgust despite the satisfaction in his eyes. I paid as much attention as anyone, I thought. The rocket had come from nowhere and caught everyone off guard. Sleep deprivation, monotony, searing heat, and the endless tinge of dread ... only the hardcore, experienced men paid attention all the time.

Some time passed. Again we sit huddled in the middle of the jungle on an ambush mission. The foliage is bathed in hues of white and grey from a full moon. Tree trunks and bushes jut upwards in different shades of dark bluish grey. It's my turn on guard. I scan the area wide-eyed and wish it was dark. I don't know who can see me. I can't see anyone but that doesn't mean they're not there. I hunker down, look at my watch and get ready for my hour on watch. I worry about the pale bath of light around me.

"Grzesik, sit up!" Sergeant Ramirez whispers. I turned to look at him. I stare. I didn't even know he was there. "Sit up, I don't want you falling asleep."

"I ain't sitting up in this light so someone out there can shoot me."

Though Ramirez had authority over me because he was a sergeant, he was not my squad or section leader. I didn't know who he was in the food chain. I didn't really care. "I said, sit up Grzesik!"

A leg slides out from underneath him like some cocked switchblade and he kicks me in my thigh. Anger and frustration well up in me and I protest again but to no avail. He kicks me again and my anger goes cold. For a second, I don't even feel like I'm in the Army. My anger now is not an anger of shame or stubbornness or even petulance. It is a deadly serious, lethal anger I feel now. Even as I lift my rifle I know the repercussions of what I'm about to do.

My arms are steady as my hands gently lift the rifle. I clasp it firmly and the safety clicks as I flip it to the fire position. The weapon protrudes from me towards Ramirez's face. Even in the dark, I can see his arrogance melt into genuine fear.

"Kick me again and I'll blow your fucking head off," I hiss.

I watch him carefully. He melts into a non-threatening blob on the jungle floor but I know I'm in trouble. This is not the first time with these sergeants. New guys like myself are always relegated to walking the point or flank position: deadly for anyone, but especially for a new guy. Besides, I didn't ask for any of this. I got drafted. I was sent here under threat of imprisonment if I didn't go. My feeling is that I am in a unit with many dishonorable superiors who look out only for themselves. Now, here I am getting kicked by one of the men I suspect have only their interests at heart. I have to escape this somehow.

The incident with Ramirez happened only a week or so after a similar run-in with my squad leader, also a sergeant. We'd been trekking across a particularly nasty piece of jungle that thickened and changed its features every few hundred feet. Small branches and tangled vines grabbed at every exposed piece of equipment I carried. At times it was so thick I thought I could fall and not hit the ground. Sometimes a lunging step would cause me to twist as vegetation grabbed a grenade or a bandage or a bandolier. My panting and heaving stopped for a second when I saw the familiar clump of leaves stuck together. Two steps ahead of me was a Weaver ant nest. We simply called them red ants. Their nests were spun and glued much like caterpillar nests back in the world. Luckily, their white streaks made them visible. The outside was covered with soldier ants who could sense a man approach before they saw him. Sprouting above a massive pair of jaws were two antennae that could sense the faintest vibration. These ants had a simple defense strategy. They were as aggressive as possible. They'd lean out and away from their perch, stretching as far as they could to immediately scamper onto, and attack any creature that touched their nest. Their jaws cut deeply. The formic acid released immediately upon the bite caused searing pain.

12. Escape

I approach the ant nest carefully. As I get to it, I swing my body, in particular my head and shoulders, around and away from it. I then turn back into a normal position and face the direction I'm walking. I miscalculate and turn too soon. The back of my pack brushes against the nest. Hundreds of ants stand upright on the nest reaching for the pack and the ones that can reach it grab onto it with their front legs and jaws. I don't know it yet but dozens of angry ants are darting quickly about my rucksack looking for exposed flesh to tear into. They find it.

The first bite sears me like a hot needle and I jump immediately. Without thinking, I throw off my pack, helmet, and rifle. I brush myself with my hands. They flail wildly about, as I get bitten repeatedly. Finally, I think I'm rid of them. I examine myself and my stuff carefully. There is nothing on my pack....

"Grzesik, what the hell are you doing?" My sergeant is there. He's angry.

"I got red ants on me," I reply defensively.

"Stop holding up the column and move your ass."

"I told you, I had red ants all over me," I protest vehemently.

"I'll see you when we get back," he answers with a menacing tone.

We walked out of there without further incident. The sun dipped behind the jungle and Dau Tieng, our base camp, welcomed us despite its menacing razor wire perimeter.

I'm sullen, despairing.... I've got more than ten months of this to go. I should be grateful to be back at base camp. Few infantry units got to operate out of the rear. To me, all it meant was a comfortable cot in a tent and a relatively secure place to sleep. I still had an eternity to serve out in this misery that I got forced into. I won't be killed by these bastards.

In my tent, the brown gloom of musty canvas envelops me. I'm putting my gear away behind my cot. Late afternoon sun floods the entrance of the tent and I'm thinking of just lying down to stare at the sloping ceiling. The sunny entrance to my tent suddenly goes black. A figure has blocked the light. I squint and see my sergeant. As my eyes adjust, I see he's rolling up his sleeves. "Grzesik, you have a problem with me?"

In one sudden jolt of awareness, I know exactly what is happening and what the probable course of this confrontation will be. I grab my machete and pull it out of its scabbard. I'm smug in the sound that it makes as I pull it out. I drop the scabbard on my cot. It lands with a low thud. I stare at him icily as I start slapping the flat side of the machete against my leg. The sergeant goes silent. Without a word, he turns and leaves. I might have hurt him or he might have punched me out if I froze. I'm thankful he had the sense to leave.

Later, I walk around Dau Tieng trying to avoid anyone from the company. Things are quickly coming to a head in this terrible unit I've been assigned to and though stoic on the outside, I'm screaming on the inside. It was all bearable till now but I know it's spun out of control. This time I pulled a rifle on a non-commissioned officer, Sgt. Ramirez, and a machete on another one. Next, they'll beat me up or court-martial me. No matter what the outcome, I'll be stuck walking point or on some dangerous listening post forever. Hell, they might even shoot me themselves in the middle of a firefight if they hate me enough. I have to get out of this place. This is the worst unit in the 25th infantry division. I'll die if I stay here.

Later that day, my platoon lieutenant approaches me. He is a country boy and a nice guy. He is well-liked, an accomplishment for an officer in Vietnam. "Grzesik, what's up with you?" His voice has charm and his cheeks are rosy. I feel empathy from him. An uncomfortable pause follows.

"Nothing, sir."

"I've been speaking to my sergeants. I can't have you pulling weapons on my NCOs. I think the best thing is for us to transfer you somewhere else." His eyes dim just a bit.

My heart raced and my vision got hazy. I didn't even remember the end of the short conversation. This could be a death sentence. This was not a random assignment. It was a reassignment for a fuck-up. Panic welled up in me but it was tempered by my strong survival instincts. I saw my deteriorating situation with new clarity. More than half my time here has been walking point or flank … or being sent out on hastily and sometimes ill-conceived forward positions. New personnel here are simply used as shields. If they don't comply, they are immediately taken into account. Two new guys have already been killed. I know many others I came in-country with are already dead. This unit does not operate in a normal military manner. It operates on the good old boy system. Anyone who has been here any time and has any rank protects himself by putting totally green men into dangerous positions. I was now my only priority. My vision to keep myself alive got clearer and more defined with every one of these events. I had to escape. Something was very wrong with this unit.

The most amazing thing about my ordeal was the simple solution to it. I talked to a few people that didn't know all my circumstances. I'd heard the rumors before. To get out of the infantry, all one had to do was re-enlist. It was that simple. All it took was an appointment with a re-enlistment guy, a quick oath, and some paperwork. With great reservations, I decided to do it.

All my fears of the re-enlistment tactic not working proved unfounded. I remember being sleepless and wishing the whole thing was done. Part of me felt that something would go wrong and I'd be back in the mess I was trying to get out of. I needed the papers with my new assignment in my hand. Only then would I feel safe.

On a bright Vietnamese morning, in the middle of the Michelin Rubber plantation, I took another oath to serve my country. Waves of relief washed over me repeatedly with each word I uttered, repeating after the enlistment officer. I felt myself being pulled further and further out of the wild spiral that I had been sucked into. Even as I sat there I could feel the vise-like grip of death breaking its hold on me. When the small ceremony was done, I finally felt free. The 2/12th Infantry leadership was glad to be rid of me and I was glad to be rid of them.

Six months passed. I found out Sergeant Ramirez got a piece of shrapnel in his ass from an RPG. He had always been a sullen, angry man. His gaze had always conveyed contempt. A mean-spirited, I'm-better-than-you-because-I'm-a-sergeant kind of guy, he never smiled and spoke condescendingly to anyone below his rank. From the start, I avoided him because my intuition told me he could be trouble. My intuition had proved right.

I was sitting on the floor of Tan Son Nhut airbase waiting to catch a ride for R&R when I first heard of it. I met one of my old comrades-in-arms from the 2/12th Infantry waiting in a boarding manifest line. He too was going on R&R. After bear hugs and laughter we sat down and caught up on events.

"You know Ramirez got wounded, He got hit in the ass by RPG shrapnel." We both laughed. My laughter was a spontaneous laughter. His was held back because he knew I would laugh first and he wanted to see it. I recalled Ramirez's words: "Maybe now you'll pay attention." Maybe he hadn't paid attention. I laughed again.

I still think of Jungle George and the other draftees I served with. Their names have faded from memory over the years. I look at their photos in my albums and their smiles shine up at me more brightly than any pictures of family or girlfriends.

13

Vung Tau to Baria

I'd finally done it. I'd found a way out of the bad infantry unit I'd been assigned to. I felt its poor leadership and policies would have killed me. My new assignment is the 36th Engineer Battalion in Vung Tau. I have a desk job, in a rear unit, in a beach resort town.

The waters of the mighty Mekong River mingle with the turquoise brine of the South China Sea just west of Vung Tau. There, the non-stop convoy of resupply ships ran up the Mekong and stuffed the belly of the military logistics machine at the Port of Saigon. Vung Tau sat close enough to Saigon to be urban, but far enough that its waters stayed clean and blue. A wide boulevard ran the length of the waterfront. Cafes and hotels dotted the mainland side and planted palms swayed at planted intervals. Offshore sea breezes quelled the normal smells associated with most Vietnamese towns. This place was clean. Fresh paint and friendly faces could easily distract one from the war raging around them. Whiskey, women, and opium were all easily obtainable here.

I processed into my new unit and talked a superior into letting me have some time to look around. I grabbed my newly issued M16, walked past the base gate, and hopped a Lambretta taxi. We headed from the base to the beach at Vung Tau. As I rode, I rejoiced in my newfound freedom and safety. My lungs heaved as I breathed the salty air and aromas of this wondrous place. A feeling of lightness replaced the tension and urgency I was so used to. I scanned the streets and avenues out of the back of the Lambretta. Just before the beach, I had the driver stop.

"How much?" I asked.

"300 Piasters."

I had my wallet in hand and was unfolding it when two street kids ran up to me. One had several hats in the hand he extended to me as I sat in the Lambretta. "Hey, GI. You want buy hat?"

I looked up at him to reply that I wasn't interested when it dawned on me that I was being hustled. I yanked my wallet out from under the hats it had been covered with. Nimble fingers had already pinched two $20 MPC notes and both kids were off and running.

At five yards I tucked my wallet under my thigh. At ten yards I grabbed my M16 and clicked the selector switch once to semi-auto. At thirty yards my rifle sights stabilized on the back of the larger kid closest to me. A smug, warm sense of satisfaction spread through me as my right index finger pulled back on the trigger. A pleasure of revenge spread through me at the prospect of shooting him dead. Slowly, my resolve faded and I released the pressure on the trigger bit by bit. I finally stood the rifle on its end but continued imagining him tumbling legs over a face skidding on concrete with blood gushing out of a gunshot wound. The little bastard was mine. I had him but I let him go. A part of me resented that charity.

To this day I wonder if that kid knew how close he came to dying. Perhaps I should have wondered then about how close I came to killing a kid. It was the second time I almost killed a civilian. Given the way the war would turn out, these incidents could have grown in my mind to enormous guilt that might have ruined me had I killed those people. Whatever guiding angel had kept me from pressing the trigger on other occasions was absent that day I rode to the beach. Perhaps he thought I should take responsibility for my own fate. A silly sentiment perhaps but I've always believed God lets go of our hand at some point and waits to see us do the right thing on our own.

The dreams began in the engineer company and would remain. I'm running through the jungle and I hear enemy voices in the background getting closer. The pounding feet pursuing me are closing in. Branches break and vegetation crunches. I awake and bolt upright in my cot in a panic.

Though I was infinitely safer here in the engineer company than I was out in the jungle with the infantry, this was still Vietnam. I always felt uneasy. The stillness and quietude unnerved me. I feared my growing complacence. A few weeks later I found out my fabulous assignment at Vung Tau was ending. D Co., 36th Engineer Battalion was relocating to Ba Ria Province to a remote basecamp consisting of tents, guard towers, and sandbags. Gone were the white sands and exotic women of Vung Tau beach. No more bars. No more PX. Overnight the reality of war stood front and center for me again though not as much for the others in the company because they'd known only easy duty.

We Had to Get Out of That Place

I was determined to get a couple of last days at the beach at Vung Tau. First I wanted to smoke some opium before making a day of it. Getting off the base was easy at Vung Tau. It sat on the end of a heavily guarded peninsula so there were few guards. Its safe location allowed it to be used as a recreation area. I hailed a cab to the edge of town, just before the beach. The opium girl I'd found lived there in a nondescript little house: small but elegant and well maintained. I never asked her name. I never needed it.

She came to the door smiling. The ritual that followed always fascinated me. I can only describe it as stylized, genteel, and as accommodating as possible. After polite conversation, she gently led me by the hand to a traditional Vietnamese polished wooden bed, complete with a wooden pillow. She waved me down with an upturned palm and sweep of her arm. She then lay down next to me and produced an opium vial and a coconut oil lamp. Twirling fingers dipped a metal rod into the vial of opium which was heated on the lamp till it hardened enough to insert into the pipe's opening. This was repeated till there was a sufficient amount of opium in the pipe. A hole was poked into the wad of opium with the metal rod. The flame of the coconut oil lamp was sucked through this hole, vaporizing the opium. This was very much a social event, one I was already familiar with. We'd discuss life, love, friends, and family. Often she'd smoke with me. War was never discussed. Opium dens were always neutral places though I never forgot I was in Vietnam.

When the smoking was done, the conversation turned slow and dreamy. During this part of the opium experience, the hard wooden platform beneath me ceased to matter. The narcotic effect of opium soothed all. The world didn't matter, nothing mattered. Staring into her captivating Oriental eyes through the euphoric cloud enveloping my senses was all that mattered. When the effect wore off slightly, very civil thanks and farewells were exchanged. The money I paid for all this always seemed minimal to me. I felt privileged to experience this social and cultural phenomenon, illegal though it was.

I left her house with a great attitude and a good buzz. Then, I headed for the beach. Vung Tau's beach had facilities to check clothing and valuables with a reasonable amount of security. I checked my stuff and walked towards the water.

I delighted in the clear mint-colored tropical waters the moment I stepped into them. They swirled warmly around my ankles. I thought of the beaches back home. These were better. These waters were warmer. They felt more welcoming. Perhaps it was the opium. Perhaps it was the respite in a war zone. Warm sun-lit breezes caressed my body as I waded into the ocean. A few steps later, through my opium haze, I felt the water lapping around my waist. This was a special moment for me, a moment of relief, release, and total relaxation. In my entire life, I had rarely felt such contentment. I lay down in the water.

I'd always been a strong swimmer. My family and all my friends spent many summers at the beach. As a kid, I could never be coaxed out of the waves. Many times my mother would pluck me, blue and shivering out of the frigid Atlantic. She'd scoop me up in a towel and force me to have something to eat. As I grew older, I'd dive headlong through the surf, and distance swimming became my primary goal. I felt a sense of peace and power bobbing in the deep-water swells. The lifeguard's stern gaze always preceded his standing on the tower and whistling at me because I was out too far. If he didn't whistle at me, I'd keep swimming further. Further into the zone of euphoria, a content feeling not unlike the one I felt now but not as strong. I considered myself un-drownable, and this was reinforced by the peak physical condition the Army had put me in.

I stroked lazily through the tropical water. I'd swum over a hundred yards. If there were lifeguards here, they didn't bother me. I felt free. Azure skies above me enhanced the peace I felt. After a while, I stopped paddling and adjusted my gaze back to the beach. The distance felt perfect. I stretched my arms and legs out and inhaled deeply. I arched my back and lay on the soft water in the gentle embrace of the South China Sea. When I exhaled water rose to the corners of my mouth. When I inhaled it receded to my cheeks. I paid attention and got into a perfect rhythm. I floated perfectly. Breathing in and out, I knew I could do this forever. The glow within me spread outwards. Mentally and physically, I felt one with the South China Sea.

After some time, I was barely aware I was in the water. My mind drifted off into happy opium-driven fantasies of my choosing. I was wherever I wanted to be. All the while, the lilting caresses of tropical waters embraced me all the more. Eventually, I was almost asleep.

I had little perception of the time passing in this euphoric state. At some point, I noticed that the arch in my back was not as comfortable as it had been. I reluctantly left my stupor and returned to a more conscious state. First I felt the water I was lying on by wiggling my fingers.

Then I became aware of it around my legs and body. I undid the arch in my back and my legs slowly sank. I gently paddled to get upright and stay afloat. I raised my head and casually gazed back towards the beach.

My eyes widened with horror as I realized there was no beach. Looking left and right, I saw only palm trees and scrub. Gone were the boulevard, the shops, and the hotels. I was looking at a primitive tropical shoreline right out of some *Gilligan's Island* nightmare. This, however, was no Gilligan's Island. This was Viet Nam and there was a real possibility of Viet Cong with guns in those trees. There was no telling where I was. I was lost and drifting with the tide. In a sudden adrenaline-driven jolt, I found myself swimming for the shore as fast as I could. The tide had moved me laterally along the shoreline but the distance to it was still about one hundred yards. I swam for all I was worth. Once I was within a hundred feet of the shore, I stood and ran sloshing onto the beach. In nothing more than my bathing suit, I ran into the wood line and leaned against a palm tree. My heart pounded in my chest. For all I knew, I was entering an endless jungle. I had no weapon, clothes, or shoes. My thoughts raced. I couldn't have drifted too far beyond civilization and roads. I had to walk a straight line through that jungle till I found a road ... or something. I presented a ridiculous sight, a skinny kid looking for an invisible enemy: like some Rambo in a bathing suit. Every so often I'd step on a twig and wince because it snapped loudly or hurt my foot. I had no idea how much time had passed when, through the scrub and trees, I saw the ribbon of a road. Relief washed over me. I gingerly stepped out of the trees, chose a direction, and started walking. To my delight and amazement, after a couple of hundred yards, I came to what was clearly an entrance to some sort of military compound. I composed myself and calmly walked in. I rounded a bend and there I saw one of the most welcome sights of my life.

Standing before me was a light-duty truck surrounded by three Caucasian males in military uniforms. They were Australians. As I sheepishly told my story, their smiles turned to guffaws and raucous laughter. They gave me a ride back to the beach at Vung Tau. I'd drifted just under a mile. I never saw that beach again after we moved to Baria Province.

Our new base camp sat positioned at the foot of a mountain, in an open field. A small South Vietnamese Army outpost about the same size as ours sat about one hundred meters from us. It afforded us some sense of security because we were only one company of men with no combat experience, out in the open, with limited weaponry. Our guys had their issued M-16's and there may have been a few M-60 machine guns in the company but little else. We didn't even have Claymore mines to use as defensive weapons on the outside of the wire that surrounded our compound. The company commander managed to get his hands on a few

Rocket type used in our makeshift perimeter defense at Baria.

crates of antiquated, large, bazooka antitank rockets and used Claymore mine detonators. He had some of our guys fashion V-shaped plywood launchers and placed the rockets in them outside the wire. The detonator wires were connected to them and ran back through the wire to our side to the inside of the perimeter. I always wondered if those rockets would fly straight and true if detonated. After all they would be fired without a bazooka tube to direct them.

Looking at these guys and our remote location, I always thought someone would get hurt and I was right. For now, the days and weeks passed without incident. Then, one day, we went to the beach (not Vung Tau). Before we left, a lieutenant approached me.

"Grzesik, you going to the beach with those guys?" The lieutenant pointed to the deuce-and-a-half truck.

"Yes, sir." I stared at him to see what was up. Officers rarely spoke to me. When they did, it usually spelled trouble ... especially when they were greenhorns.

"Grab your rifle and ride shotgun. Somebody should have a weapon on that truck."

He was absolutely right, of course. The naivete and lack of combat experience in the engineer company concerned me but that was exactly why I was there. I'd clawed my way out of the infantry because of the growing premonition I'd be killed in combat. I still believed that.

I was always concerned that if we did come under attack, the majority of these guys would be useless. They had almost no combat training and no experience in it. There was little enemy activity here in Ba Ria province. Vung Tau served as an R&R spot for American troops even though many Viet Cong operated there due to its proximity to Saigon. This was their turf. The peace was on their terms. The calm here always felt like the calm before the storm.

Without saying a word I turned and walked across our small compound to my hooch. I grabbed my M16, a bandolier of ammo, and raced back to the truck.

"Somebody hold this." My arm reached up with my rifle before I climbed up. A hand shot out and grabbed it for me. The motor had been running while they waited for me and the truck lurched forward, gears grinding, as soon as the tailgate slammed shut. My feet hadn't steadied yet and my buttocks slammed the bench as I lost my footing. I stuck my rifle between my legs, balancing myself, and looked up defensively. I was the guy that was going to be looking out for the rest of them. They were too cherry to look after themselves. I thought of the lieutenant's words. Blank eyes stared at me and it occurred to me that one man with a rifle protecting a truckload of men was no protection at all in Vietnam. Everybody on that truck should have had a rifle.

The truck bounced past the barbed wire, out of the compound, and turned right. A mile of rural dirt road populated with pedestrians, motorcycles, and water buffalo led to the main highway that stretched to the beach east of there. I thought about the time I'd tried driving a Lambretta motorcycle on one of these roads and almost hit one of those buffalo...

Fifteen minutes later, around the halfway point of our trip, green fields and rice paddies gave way to an even greener forest. Signs of civilization faded as the number of dwellings and huts zipping by us decreased. Soon we rumbled through nothing but forest. I looked at the guys. I smiled and I thought that t-shirts and shorts hardly looked like war zone attire. The woods on the left side of the truck now looked like so many woods I'd taken fire from while in the infantry. On an impulse, I stood up, raised my rifle to my shoulder, and fired a full magazine on full auto, into the woods. Everyone looked at me, their eyes surprised or quizzical. A grin spread on my face.

We made it to the beach, swam, ate, and mingled with the populace. We took pictures and drank warm Vietnamese beer. It was good to have sun on our faces and be away from it all. Our return to base was simply another uneventful bumpy ride on the road we'd come on. The day had been a relaxing respite from the drudgery of our routines.

About a week passed and I was called into the company commander's office. "Grzesik I want you to escort the bodies of Mallard and McLellan to the mortuary in Saigon." His eyes left the paperwork on his desk and looked up at me.

"You do know that their jeep was hit by a landmine on the main coastal road, right?"

"The road to the beach?" I asked.

"Yes."

For years I've wondered if I had anything to do with their death. I've never really felt any guilt. Was I too reckless firing my M16? Of course. But these things happen in war all the time and I knew that. I have, however, on many occasions walked around that black pit of the guilt I'd shed myself of, and peered into it attempting to see if any of it still belonged to me.

14

Baria to Vinh Long

It became apparent to me and everyone else in the engineer company that I had very limited skills for the job I'd been thrust into. My reenlistment choice had been draftsman, but the only relevant ability I had in that area was some calligraphy I'd picked up here and there. I could print a title and information on a blueprint, but there was no one to teach me the mechanical drawing involved; after all, this was a war zone. Eventually, after being seen too many times with nothing to do, I was put on a road crew. I didn't have much choice in the matter. Thankfully, this duty was easy compared to the infantry. I wasn't counting down my days in dread as I had been in the infantry, though the idea of being out in the open again concerned me.

Every morning we rode out of our base camp on trucks to maintain the roads leading to and around Baria province. I got to know the area pretty well and after a while felt comfortable enough to engage the locals in conversation. As usual, kids ran out to sell us souvenirs or warm cokes with chunks of ice. I was comfortable letting my guard down somewhat but never left my rifle far away. Once I bought a Coke and had no way to open it. On a whim, I decided to shoot a hole in the top edge of the can. I knew it wouldn't work but I did it anyway. Foam flew in all directions and only a gulp was left by the time I grabbed the spinning can.

A blaring sun rose in the sky and the heat of the afternoon settled on us like a weight. We'd patch one section of the road and move by truck to another. The road from Vung Tau started with beach sand on one side and bay on the other. Five or six miles in, as the road curved inland, the ocean side transitioned to mangroves and was uninhabitable. The bay side receded to mangroves and lagoons interspersed with hamlets and marketplaces. Further still, everything spread out into solid land with glistening rice paddies patch-worked with earthen dykes.

I'd been running the ground compactor and it was time to take a break. My arms were getting numb from the vibration so I handed the machine off to another guy. I grabbed my weapon, lit a cigarette, and leaned against our truck. I'd been watching a shirtless man in black shorts on the other side of the road working in the muck of the lagoon there. Now I paid more attention. I watched him push his elongated spade into the thick mud of the canal edge. With an even greater effort, he pulled away the slice of the bank he had cut. With a heave, he slung it over his shoulder to a growing pile beyond the top of the bank. He stood knee-deep in the lagoon water.

He worked bent over using both hands in the typical digging motion even though there was little shank between the handle and the blade. The canal bank he was excavating sat half-exposed in the water. Off to the left, a crude canoe rocked slowly in the water. Above it, a roughly hewn wooden walkway led to a small house further down and around the bank.

I watched fascinated. I imagined he might take the discarded material to bake in a kiln later to make bricks or that perhaps he was removing shoreline to create a larger lagoon: maybe both. These people wasted nothing. The tool he used seemed to be handmade. I could tell by the rough-cut wood of the handle, and the crude hammered look of the blade, the tool hadn't been made in any factory. This man was of the peasant class. I surmised that most of the things he owned were made by hand.

The children here wore a lot of white, especially on top, while the rest of the people in this hamlet mostly wore the traditional black pajamas so often associated with the Viet Cong. In fact, this was the peasant style across the country and most Vietcong were peasants. Educated people in the cities and landowners dressed in western or traditional clothes. They did not have black-stained teeth from chewing betel nuts as peasants throughout the countryside did. Their skins were not dark from labor in the sun. This was the dichotomy that was Vietnam. This was part of the class difference that fueled the class war in Vietnam.

The laborer's motions repeated with clockwork precision. His body worked in a perfect rhythm: thrust, lift, heave. I looked down at my watch and then at him. Every motion lasted approximately two seconds. Thrust, lift, heave ... he seemed to never tire because his sinewy arms and forearms worked like a clock mechanism. It occurred to me I could never match his stamina and endurance. I went back to work.

Villagers on the road to Baria.

Market on the road to Baria.

We moved to our next stop. There was another building similar to the last one we saw on that side of the road. A ramp on stilts led to what was an outhouse of sorts over the water of the lagoon. As I worked I saw movement from the corner of my eye. A man walked out of the house down the ramp to the outhouse to do his business. The guys with me had slowed down and happened to look towards him. We were simply curious about the odd set-up over the water. As the man relieved himself the lagoon came alive with fish. There were hundreds of them. The moving mass-created waves rose almost a foot high. Enough fish swirled in that lagoon to feed the village. Maybe they did feed the village. We couldn't stop laughing.

Working here on this road offered me another perspective of the people of South Vietnam. I could study them casually. Unhurried, spontaneous conversation was possible more often than it had been on combat operations. These people were very good-natured and possessed a surprising sophistication of wit. There was a very cordial mischievousness about them. Fantastic sights availed themselves to us regularly. At one point I saw lizard-like fish ... perhaps they were fish-like lizards ... they'd walk right out of the mangrove swamp water and up onto the bank. On one stretch of the road with markets and concrete buildings, I saw a woman balancing two round trays of dead dogs she was taking to market on a stick over her shoulder. The Vietnamese ate dogs. Oddly, the two round trays reminded me of Lady Liberty's scales of justice.

Days passed smoothly on the road. Then weeks...

The sun dropped towards the mangroves in the distance. It was late afternoon. Light glinted off the rice paddy between the stalks. We had finished work for the day and were returning to our base camp. Standing in the bed of our truck we relished the breeze as we bounced along the road. Driving east we noticed multiple army vehicles and men stopped ahead. Something was up. We approached cautiously. It looked like a truck in the rice paddy from a distance. Then I thought I was looking at wheels on top of the truck instead of underneath. Seconds later I realized it was an overturned fuel truck in the rice paddy on the right side of the road. Men stood gathered together off the road, on the edge of the paddy near the area of the cab, and peered down into it. One man stood in the water, bent and reaching into the truck cab. The driver was stuck in the cab of the overturned truck and he was trying to get him out.

Our driver pulled over immediately. We dismounted and ran towards the overturned truck and I was able to get within ten feet of the cab. I looked at the men standing around me to get a sense of what was being done to address the situation. I wanted to see if I could help. Everyone had the same intense but vacant stare. I turned back to the truck helpless. There was nothing I could do. I simply stared, like everyone else. Looking closer I realized the truck was sinking in the muck of the rice paddy. Ten seconds earlier I had seen the top of the driver's shoulders and now only his head was visible. His pleading screams filled the air though they made no sense. Someone yelled, "The water is rising around the cab." We all looked at each other and then back to the truck.

Now the eyes of the man in the truck appeared glazed and non-seeing. Gas fumes, noxious, sweet, and pungent, had overcome him. They wafted into the tropical air and made breathing difficult. The water of the paddy shimmered with prismatic colors as gasoline expanded over its surface. The would-be rescuer started talking frantic gibberish: he was being overcome by the gasoline fumes as well. He was beginning to garble his words and make pleading sounds. Another man immediately took over for him. Now only the trapped man's face showed above the water in the truck cab. It looked like a grisly mask floating on the surface.

"Tell that man to put his cigarette out!" The shouted words thudded through us like a bolt of lightning. A lit cigarette?

No ... no...

All heads turned towards the source of the voice and time stood still. Then, there was only one movement among our stunned still bodies. A single man's head cocked downwards to look at the lit cigarette in his hand as he simultaneously extended his arm to flick the cigarette with his middle finger. We all watched that cigarette helplessly as it flew tumbling end over end in perfect mid-air revolutions. The cigarette that would ignite the gasoline in the water and incinerate all of us.

It hit the gasoline atop the rice paddy water and simply hissed briefly as it went out.

Shortly afterward the man was pulled free. The truck remained in the rice paddy until a piece of heavy equipment could haul it out the next day. We drove through the open barbed wire gate of our base camp around five o'clock and headed for our hooches and makeshift showers. That night, I slept well. It had been a good day and I'd done a good day's work.

In the morning I woke refreshed. After chow, I headed towards the truck the guys usually met up at to work on the road. On the way, I saw the company clerk and a few of his friends walking towards me. All had their M16 rifles. I heard them engaged in animated conversation.

"Where you guys coming from?" I asked

"Oh, just a little hunting expedition." The company clerk smirked and looked at his friends with a knowing smile.

"Oh yeah? What did you guys hunt?" I persisted.

"Dogs out back." He didn't like being questioned.

In Vietnam, American bases always attracted dogs. Our compound in the middle of nowhere was no different. Though we burned our garbage daily, remnants of foodstuffs lingered in the air. A pack of dogs numbering about seven had started running the area behind our compound. The captain wanted something done about it and the company clerk eagerly obliged. He and his cohorts baited the dogs into a group and then ambushed them with rifle fire.

Though I knew there was an Army regulation somewhere that justified this, and even mandated it, I could not help but feel some contempt. They had enjoyed it way too much. The clerk read my mind. His eyes narrowed.

"Grzesik, you got guard tonight," he said.

Company clerks were among the most powerful people in any unit.

"Oh yeah? Says who?" I replied angrily.

"The lieutenant. Branson's sick or something so you got it."

"I just pulled guard three nights ago ... fuckin' shit."

"You're on the back tower with Pineapple. Go pick up the crystal ball from the CO."

I turned and walked sullenly. That night, after I'd worked all day, I went to the captain's hooch around six p.m. Once there I announced myself. We rarely saluted in Vietnam because it could make a target of the person being saluted.

"Sir, I have guard tonight. I'm here to pick up the Starlight Scope."

I could see the case containing the scope next to the safe. His eyes followed mine to the scope. His arm reached out towards it but he suddenly pulled it back.

"You know the protocol?"

"Yes, sir. Don't let it fall into enemy hands under any circumstances. I know because I used one while I was in the infantry."

He eyed me for a few seconds before reaching for the case again to hand to me. I could tell he thought I was a know-it-all. He looked to be from a Northeast college. Though now in the military, he still possessed some preppy schoolboy looks. The words of Samuel Adams came to mind when I saw him eyeing the Combat Infantryman's Badge on my chest: "Men think meanly of themselves for never having gone to war or been at sea."

"Thank you, sir." I turned and walked out.

Sleep deprivation had always been an Achilles heel for me and it always happened with guard duty. I'd never been able to function correctly without the proper amount of sleep. For me, that was a minimum of six hours. In Vietnam, we slept in shifts on guard duty. Whether through gunfire or artillery, we were expected to function the next day. The actual amount of sleep men got in the field varied between three to six hours, by my estimation. Often in combat, they got none. Some men developed a gaunt black-eyed appearance. The look eventually was labeled "the thousand-yard stare."

I sat in that guard tower yet another night. The Hawaiian known as Pineapple was a good guy to pull guard with. We'd whisper and laugh till one of us took his turn to sleep. Even in the dark, I could see the speckles on his face where he'd burned himself. He'd been tasked with taking loads of garbage out beyond the perimeter and burning them with diesel fuel. Young kid that he was, he never knew the difference between diesel fuel and gasoline. In his mind, they both burned so gasoline would be okay. When he lit the match, he was blown nine feet into the grass behind him. The instant flash had seared only the outer layers of his skin.

Darkness always came with its shadows and demons. Sometimes they were real, sometimes imagined. After a while, phantasms of darkness appeared to move. Sometimes I wondered if the shadow I was looking for had been there five minutes earlier. Of course, I knew my eyes were playing tricks on me but I couldn't be sure. Staring into tangled darkness hard enough caused imagination to blend with reality.

Sleep, if I was allowed any, was always difficult for me after those lonely nights on guard duty. Hours of imagining bogeymen in the night played havoc on my psyche. I'd lie down wide-eyed, trying to shut out the other-worldly catatonia that set in after peering into the dark for hours. For me, the feeling upon waking was like an extreme jet lag ... a dragging fatigue of the body and mind that lasted well into the coming day.

Three days later, I'm on guard duty again on the tower. It's quiet. There have been no signs of the enemy since I got here. The night is still. Nothing stirs, not even mosquitoes. I sit cradled by sandbags and I recline to look upward, my rifle never far from me. Though I am tired, I don't want to go to sleep. I am at peace. So many bright stars above me; more than I have ever seen before, render a calm I rarely feel anymore. This temporary serenity could only give way to a troubled sleep anyway. I'd rather just sit here and look at the stars. The display overhead shifts delicately across the sky. If I'm still enough and breathe slowly, I can see the entire array of the cosmos I'm watching move to the left. It is as though time is speeding up. Or is it slowing down?

A streak of light, far above me, jerks me away from my spell-bound gaze. At the same time, I see a new spot of light in the sky. I stare at it. It seems to be brighter than everything else around it.

I look at the area where I saw the streak. Whatever it was, it was faster than a meteor. Is that possible? I look back at the spot of light and squint hard. I think it is rounder, with a more defined edge than the stars around it. It is definitely circular. As I stare, it streaks away. Faster than I can see, the spot just disappears and streaks as it did before. I can't be sure because it is so fast. It reappears at a different point of the sky just as suddenly. By my estimation, it moved seventy degrees in a one-hundred-and-eighty-degree horizon. My thoughts coalesce to a quick conclusion. Whatever it is I am looking at is far above the earth, in the edges of space or beyond, and it just moved from a still position to a speed far beyond any capable of being achieved by man-made technology. It did so without any discernible acceleration ... it achieved full speed without having to speed up. Furthermore, it stopped the same way. My high school physics classes come to mind. The energy needed to overcome the inertia in that object, whether starting it or stopping it, should have turned it into molecular dust. What I am seeing defies fundamental scientific laws of motion and inertia. The object disappears in another streak, and though I eagerly look for it, it does not return.

I slowly withdraw from the wonder I have just seen and carefully peer into the darkness beyond the barbed wire. I haven't been paying attention and Charlie could be out there.

I am beginning to get weary of all the guard duty I have to pull. As a resentful draftee, it is my right. I have found a clever way to get time off. Going on sick call to see a doctor requires a trip to Vung Tau. Arranging a meeting with a specialist puts me in Long Binh, which is a short drive to Saigon with its bars and women. I convinced doctors a couple of times to make appointments for me to see them. The first time I did this

95

I planned poorly. I got to Vung Tau, got an appointment to see a specialist, and was told there would be no helicopter to Long Binh till eight am. I walked around the base trying to find a place to bed for the night when I saw a guy with a CIB (Combat Infantry Badge) and a 25th Division patch. I still wore mine wore on my right shoulder in addition to my 36th Engineer patch. We shook hands and I told him my situation. He grinned at me. I knew right away I'd lucked out.

"Man, I got a place for you to crash." He laughed, "It's on the floor in the morgue where I work. It is right next to the chopper pad."

"That's cool," I replied. "I'm used to sleeping in the jungle in six inches of water so concrete's no biggy. I'll get us some beer."

"Yeah, we can have a couple but we have to be cool."

We drank till the late evening and reminisced about our time fighting with the 25th. The next morning I woke to men's voices, clanging sounds, and a rush of cold air next to me. I opened my eyes to see a lieutenant standing over me.

"Who is this man?" he said while never breaking eye contact with me.

I immediately answered for my new buddy.

"Sir, I have to catch an important flight to Long Binh so I spent the night here."

"The body in there is a dead man who died of tuberculosis and rabies. You have to get rabies shots." He pointed to the refrigerated compartments I'd been sleeping next to.

I looked over and saw one of the doors was wide open. Inside lay a small body shrouded with a cloth. Rabies: I thought about the long painful series of shots in the stomach I'd have to endure. Then I heard the helicopter landing on the pad. "Sir, that's my bird," I announced as I jumped up. I sprinted away hoping he wouldn't follow. He didn't, and I flew away on that beautiful bird.

When I got back to the company, a couple of days later, no questions were asked. They never were, but the penance I paid for my slacking was guard duty that very night. In the morning, as I walked exhausted back to my hooch, one of the guys approached me. "Grzesik, we're going out on a patrol out back of the perimeter. We're going to walk past that field and up the mountain. You want to come help us out?"

"Sure, give me a minute," I answered.

It felt good that they'd asked me. They knew I had experience in the field. Though I didn't know these guys well, they apparently knew me. I couldn't refuse them and I wouldn't have anyway. It would have looked cowardly. My very next thought was of us walking up on an enemy observation team near the base of that mountain and them killing us all.

The company was in the middle of yet another move to a new base camp, this time to Vinh Long to the south in the Delta. Our unit strength had diminished significantly because the majority of our men had left with equipment and trucks. The idea of reconning the area around us made sense. It was possible that the enemy could be watching us or possibly worse; he could be planning to take advantage of our downsized situation to attack.

We walked to the front of the compound and then out and around the barbed wire. Then we walked along the side of our compound till it ended. Ahead of us the field spread towards the mountain. I felt like I was in the infantry again. Our patrol consisted of eight men. I let one of them take the lead. I positioned myself in the middle of our hastily formed team so I could communicate with anyone quickly if I had to. I told everyone to stay far apart from each other.

We began walking through the field I had seen so many times on guard duty and after a couple of hundred yards, the ground beneath us began sloping upward. The field we had passed had no trees but as we began our ascent, the vegetation changed and we were soon among scattered small trees. I looked back at our base camp and it had diminished to a distant square. We were one-third of the way up the mountain. As we continued our ascent the number of trees increased. There were enough of them now to hide an enemy presence.

Our lead man stopped. He looked down at the ground at something. "Don't touch it," I blurted out loudly not knowing if these guys knew about booby-traps.

The guys in the front began discussing something and the word filtered down to me that I was needed there. I climbed up quickly hoping that they had not found unexploded ordnance or a booby trap. I approached the lead man.

"Grzesik, what's this?" He pointed at the base of the tree where I saw a stick in the ground with a simple noose attached to it.

"It's a trap," I said.

"You mean a snare," he responded with a laugh. He was right. It was a snare, not a trap. Being a Southern boy he knew how to make distinctions that were beyond a New York City boy like myself. I'd seen makeshift devices like this before; snares on land and fish traps in creeks and ponds. They usually consisted of sticks or sticks with rope. The enemy used any food resource he could find. I looked up at the guys.

"It's a snare, all right. Guess who put it there?" I stared at them and they stared back wide-eyed. I decided it was a bad idea to proceed any further. We turned and descended back towards our basecamp.

Two days later, what remained of us was taken by truck to a Navy port where we all loaded onto an LST for the remainder of the journey to our new base at Vinh Long.

Our trip up the Mekong River proved to be memorable though it was relatively short. No one sat inside the hulking World War II-era ship. We all sat along the rails relishing the sights of Vietnam. Many of our guys had never taken a boat ride before. Even I, a regular on the large party fishing boats in New York City, was enchanted with the view. When we entered a narrower portion of the river that had thick foliage on its banks, a Navy guy told us to duck below the railings for protection because they sometimes took fire there. He told us their boat could not return fire because their weapons were too large and there was a village behind the vegetation. One second later, the rails of the entire ship clanked in unison as our weapons went up on them. I looked up at the sailor who had given us the briefing. He was grinning from ear to ear. When we got to a wide section of the river again, the Navy fed us rabbit for lunch. It tasted like chicken.

We disembarked at the Navy port at Vinh Long and drove straight to the main base there. We never got to go off the base after that. Vinh Long was as big a base as I'd seen since Cu Chi. It had everything we needed including the largest mess hall I'd seen in Vietnam. To this day, the best blueberry pancakes I ever ate in my life were made by the Army cooks at Vinh Long.

Being already familiar with Saigon, I'd go there when traveling for legitimate reasons such as reporting to R&R, escorting bodies to the mortuary, or between assignments. Strategically speaking, I usually had about a day to party hard or do whatever I wanted. Anything longer than that could raise eyebrows. If anyone questioned a timeline or a date on orders, the logical question would be, "Where were you?" The guaranteed follow-up would question where the night was spent. At that point, a person could be on dangerous ground. He would probably be suspected of being AWOL, a potentially serious crime. I took advantage of one more opportunity to get to Saigon.

Not many people ever got to see Saigon. I was lucky. During two tours I got to go at least six times. I never passed up an opportunity. I'd seen cities in Europe and I'd been in Canada and throughout the United States but Saigon held a fascination for me. The word exotic is usually used to describe cities in this region of the world but I prefer the word "mysterious." Wherever I traveled in that town, I always craned my head to see around the next block. Shadowy figures in doorways beckoned by hand if they didn't speak English. They always had something they wanted me to come and see. It could be women, it could be drugs or it could be a trap. I always suspected that if a person was careless enough he might never be seen again.

Saigon was the capital of Vietnam and many enemy operatives lurked in its shadows. I got approached a few times by people asking if I had greenbacks (American dollars). They always looked a little bit apprehensive and had an air of danger around them. Trading in dollars was illegal for anyone, including the Vietnamese. Simply possessing them was illegal for Americans and probably the Vietnamese also. Dollars were used extensively in the black market and those who could get away with dealing in them made small fortunes. I had a gut feeling that these illegal American dollars funded the enemy. I'd buy liquor and cigarettes for the mammasans at the PX as a favor, but I never dealt in illegal currency for that reason.

The area of Cho Lon, right outside the main airbase had everything I could want, and I usually didn't venture much past it, but on one occasion I hired a cyclo to take me around the town. A cyclo was a bench seat with two wheels attached to a bicycle frame. They traversed the roads around Saigon and were used by the populace, visitors, and soldiers alike. They were a good way to take in the sights and sounds of Saigon if one cared to forgo the wild side and partake in an effortless, pleasant, sightseeing ride through the city. Camera and rifle in hand, I told the driver to take me around and show me the sights of Saigon.

We weaved through traffic and the teeming streets of Saigon. The driver expertly peddled the cyclo between cars. There seemed to be an unspoken courtesy between motorized vehicles and cyclos. I was a little nervous because I was essentially a human bumper. Only the metal rails and slabs of wood my feet rested on stood between me and the rest of the traffic. I eased into the ride after a while and relaxed, taking in the sights. We passed bustling open-air markets, multicolored and beautifully terraced apartment buildings, and peaceful tree-lined streets. Beautiful women dressed in traditional Vietnamese ao dais strolled delicately through the streets. Some carried umbrellas and most had silken bluish-black hair down to their waist. The civilized quiet bustle of this city gave me the impression it was more sophisticated than most cities in the United States. At one point we passed the Saigon zoo. Swirling ornate concrete edifices adorned its perimeter. I saw an intricately carved, serpentine dragon. One would never know there was a war going on here.

Suddenly, on my right side, the streets seemed to clear of trees and structure. Fewer people walked on the streets. A couple of hundred yards away a large white building dominated the landscape. It took me a second to recognize it. The handsomely constructed, pristine concrete building before me was the presidential palace. I told the cyclo driver to stop. Before me stood the seat of power in Vietnam. It represented and stood for all I was fighting for. This building held the offices of the president of Vietnam, and the highest commanders of his military.

I sat there in awe on that cyclo. Suddenly, I noticed the driver was very nervous. I completely understood why and I told him that we would leave in a minute. I raised my camera and began taking pictures.

From nowhere a Vietnamese policeman appeared. He demanded my camera with an outstretched arm and a shrill voice. Though he

Photograph taken of the Presidential Palace before being accosted by a Vietnamese policeman.

spoke Vietnamese, I understood what he was saying. In Vietnam, soldiers called Vietnamese cops "white mice" because of their tiny stature, white uniform, and noncombatant status. Thoughts and rationalizations raced through my head. I was fighting for this man's country and my friends were dying here. I was not giving this white mouse my camera and I let him know by shaking my head. He screamed at me again and put his hand on the .38 caliber revolver he wore on his waist. Rage welled up in me as I grabbed my M16 and pointed it at his mid-section. His eyes widened and his hand fell from the pistol. We both turned and left while we had the chance. That episode ended my last foray into the capital city. My tour of Vietnam was winding down to a close, though I was nowhere close to an Army discharge date. I would miss this place but I would see it again, I just didn't know it yet ... and then my tour ended. I boarded a jet for thirty days' leave in New York City.

15

Kiss Panama Goodbye

After a blissful leave, I reported two weeks late to my new duty station, the 3rd Armored Cavalry in Fort Lewis. I didn't care. I'd just gotten back from Vietnam and I had at least two years left to go in the Army. My reenlistment had gotten me out of the infantry in Vietnam, but it had also extended my time in the service. What I didn't know was that after Vietnam, I would never fit into military structure again though I never really had to begin with. To my surprise, I found my new cavalry unit easy-going and composed. Cadre always had their problems with the men but that was to be expected anywhere in the military. Though I had earned little rank, the CIB on my chest commanded some respect. I only needed a small amount of that because I never felt I earned more than a little. This unit was quickly filling up with bona fide war heroes. A lot of guys were coming back from Vietnam with medals and sergeant stripes. I respected these men more than they knew because I never felt I was made of the same stuff.

It was April 1969 and the summer of love two years earlier had left its mark. Hippies roamed the cities from San Diego to Seattle. Fleetwood Mac, Santana, and Lee Michaels were all the rage and played in Seattle just down the highway from the barracks. Natural beauty surrounded me. In the east, Mount Rainier towered over three miles high. Out behind our motor pool lay a crystal-clear lake in a forest alive with wildlife. On the other side of the base flowed the Nisqually River where I caught my first salmon. I quickly came to appreciate the fact that life was good in the 3rd Armored Cavalry. I felt calm, I no longer felt I was always running. I fit in pretty well and made friends. Being in the Army here felt like a regular nine-to-five job. I wore clean form-fitting fatigues with crisp creases and fresh patches every day. I always chose them heavily starched and the resulting feeling was similar to wearing office clothing. I found one

Park in Saigon.

could easily stand out in a sea of green uniforms by being the best dressed.

Seattle was our usual destination on the weekends. I look back and wonder how we all survived those drunken drives back to Ft. Lewis. On one occasion I worked the gas pedal on a Road Runner while my friend drove and worked the brakes. We even got pulled over for speeding and then let go. There were sober adventures as well. Washington State's vistas of ocean and mountains sprawled endlessly. Taking advantage of the natural splendor around me, I'd fish the pristine streams and bays. Some guys hunted. I'd rent small motorboats and putter out into Puget Sound where the current was sometimes stronger than the ability of the motor to move the boat.

Once we dropped an artillery simulator overboard to kill fish. I'd heard of it being done in Vietnam. I'd been assigned, during one of our combat exercise maneuvers, to set off a few of these artillery simulators. They were low-grade explosive training devices used to mimic combat explosions. They were, however, powerful enough to take off a hand or an arm. Once again I'd been picked for my combat experience, this time for handling explosives. I used two of the small bombs but saved one for

103

myself. I brought it with us the day Bobby and I went fishing. Despite my tying it to a sinker and wrapping it very well with fishing line, the simulator came loose and floated right back up to the top of the water a few seconds later. It sizzled and spun in the water and to my abject horror, only six inches from the boat. It could have blown a hole in the boat and sunk us had I not immediately started the engine. The Coast Guard came within minutes because of the loudness of the explosion. Our Army haircuts gave us away, and almost immediately the Coast Guard guys knew we were responsible for the blast, though they could not prove it.

"Where are you guys from?" one asked.

"Fort Lewis," I replied as poker-faced as I could.

Two of them glared at us while the remaining one drove their boat away. Bobby and I ended the day laughing about it all. On another occasion when I rented one of those motorboats, a killer whale came up fifty yards away from me. Tons and tons of wild sea beast stared down at me coldly through a surprisingly small but intently staring eye. At that time the Navy manuals warned of killer whales. I thought I might be a dead man till he disappeared below the surface and swam off. Those days in the sun on Puget Sound would always lie easy on my mind. The rest of the time, I waited for my enlistment to be over and wondered how I could hasten it. Then one day, after company formation, the company clerk approached me.

"Grzesik, would you be interested in an assignment in Panama?"

"Maybe. It would depend on what I'm doing there."

"There's a jungle warfare training school down there and they need instructors. You qualify because you're a jungle combat vet with a lot of time left till you ETS."

"I'm in."

"Okay, I'll send the battalion clerk to see you but it'll cost you fifty bucks."

Our illegal conversation ended with shifty eyes and a nod. A week later I'd almost forgotten about it. That kind of talk was cheap in the Army. Then, one morning after formation, our company clerk told me to expect the battalion clerk and have the money ready. Just like that, I had a new assignment.

The hardest part of getting to Panama was "clearing post" at Fort Lewis before going on leave. I had to get clearances from the library, the PX, the Fort Lewis Army band, and scores of other organizations to show that I didn't have any money or property outstanding. Orders in hand, I walked around the base the entire day before I was finished. By then, it was late in the afternoon. To my thinking, there was no point in attempting my journey at the end of the day. I decided to stay in the barracks overnight though I was officially on leave for thirty days before reporting for duty in Panama. I slept in my bunk that night, as I had for almost a year. In the morning I woke with the rest of the guys. When they went downstairs for morning formation, I stayed in the barracks and packed my duffel bag. Afterward, I went downstairs to get some breakfast in the mess hall. Then, I was going to be on my way.

The chow line stretched down the hall from the mess hall entrance. Just outside the door stood a small stand with a booklet on it. It was meant to be signed as we entered the mess hall. I'd done this for a year and never thought about the reason for it so I bent over and signed it as usual.

"Grzesik, you're on separate rations because you're on leave. You're supposed to pay for your meal." I looked towards the voice to see a lieutenant speaking to me.

I simply nodded my head and walked into the chow hall. No one liked this particular lieutenant and no one took him seriously. He was fresh out of West Point and rumor had it his wife was cheating on him with a sergeant. He had the angry defensive persona of a man in that position and we believed the rumors. I knew he was technically correct about the separate rations status but I also knew that it was the sort of thing no one enforced. Guys on separate rations ate in the mess hall occasionally, especially during exercises or inspections, and often didn't have any chance to pay. I quickly ate and left the chow hall. As I turned the corner in the double doorways of the mess hall, I saw the lieutenant again.

"Grzesik, you didn't pay for your meal. Report to the captain."

I looked him in the eye, then I turned and left feeling anger and frustration.

"I said report to the captain!" He grabbed my left arm and pulled back spinning me into a perfect position for me to punch him with my raised fist. His face blanched and he stepped back. I trotted upstairs quickly to get my packed duffel bag, but I knew I'd done it. There was no way of getting out of this one.

Our barracks sat on a cul-de-sac of sorts and I thought that if I grabbed my bag and ran quickly, I might catch one of the cabs that circled the base there. I bounded to the top of the stairs, ran into my barracks dorm, grabbed my stuff, and ran downstairs. Then I raced out of one of the side doors towards the road. Deep down I knew I wasn't going to make it and I was surprised to have gotten that far. I was still fifty feet from the road when I heard them.

"Run, Grzesik, run!"

"Go! Goooooooo!"

I looked over my shoulder back at the building and saw the heads of my company guys sticking out the windows waving, yelling, and rooting for me to escape. At the same time, I saw the same door I had just come out of open again. Out came the lieutenant with a sergeant I knew and liked. He was wearing a .45 pistol. It was all over. I simply put my bag down. As the two approached me I could see the lieutenant was enraged. I could tell the sergeant didn't want to be there by his downward gaze.

"Sorry Grzesik, I don't want to do this, but I have to," he said.

I knew I could kiss Panama goodbye. I was placed under arrest and forced to sleep in the orderly room under armed guard. Every day the specter of the stockade weighed heavily on my mind but I was never sent there. Thankfully, the captain, a veteran of the 11th Armored Cavalry in Vietnam, had sympathy for my plight. He let me continue staying in the orderly room while he decided what to do with me but I always had an armed guard on me after duty hours. I believe he had no choice in the matter since one of his junior officers instituted the charges.

At one point on a Friday night, my guard got angry that he had not been replaced. He'd been counting on leaving for the weekend. He put his .45 pistol down in a fit of anger and said, "Guard yourself." When he left, I took the weapon and walked upstairs. The seats in the dayroom were packed. They always were for *Star Trek*. I threw the pistol and holster into the first lap with a friendly face and announced, "You're my guard."

Senator Jacob Javits of New York State intervened on my behalf because of a letter my friend the company armorer had written him regarding my illegal confinement. The charges against me were dropped that Monday morning. It was easy for the captain to do this because the lieutenant had just been shipped out to Vietnam.

Now it was time to move on. My ETS date was still a year off and I had to keep moving lest my penchant for trouble again cross paths with the proverbial piper to pay. My currency of luck was long expended. Vietnam seemed like a good choice. I was good at manipulating authority so I figured a second tour there in a unit of my choosing would be a good way to whittle down my remaining time. Usually, people on second or multiple tours got some say in their choice of assignment. I imagined some clerk position. I'd gotten good at two-finger typing at Fort Lewis.

After another 30 day leave, when I arrived for my second tour of Vietnam, I was informed by the intake clerk that job choice for people doing multiple tours was no longer a policy. "We have too many clerks," he said as he smugly eyed me. I would be assigned according to my MOS (Military Occupational Specialty). My heart sank. I was back in the fire.

16

F Company Rangers

Despite all my effort and success at staying out of the infantry and those deadly jungles, I was headed there again, this time by my own doing. Though I was just a young, scatterbrained kid making impulse decisions, they somehow turned out to be the right decisions. I felt resigned but not fearful and that surprised me. After all the effort I put into getting out of the infantry on my first tour, here I was on a second tour, going back to it again. Somehow I felt it would all work out. I was two years older now. Though not much older than before, I was no longer a fresh-faced recruit. The Army had matured me in many ways. I figured even if I wound up in an infantry unit, I'd be a lot more suited to it now. I was determined never to let anyone push me around again once I got to my assigned unit. I'd make sure I was not worth the trouble of hassling with. I steeled myself mentally and I was not too concerned.

Once again I was assigned to the 25th Division. On the second day of in-country orientation, I noticed a sign by the instructor's board while sitting in the bleachers. It was a small sign and I hadn't noticed it the day before. It depicted a man's head wearing a beret. The face was streaked black and green with camouflage paint. It simply read, "Apply for the Rangers."

Everything fell into place at once. I had experience and I was no longer a lowly private. This was a chance for military stardom. If I died I wouldn't die plodding in the mud endlessly taking pointless orders for a lost cause. Most of America disagreed with this war but I agreed with it. In my mind, it wasn't that complicated. We were trying to stop Communists from overrunning South Vietnam. My instincts also told me this could be a great adventure as well so I decided to apply. Immediately after the orientation, I walked over to the Ranger compound. Even as I approached it I could tell the place was special. All the buildings were painted in the black and yellow colors of the Rangers. In the distance, a rappelling tower overshadowed the compound. Men milled about and they walked in a distinct shoulders back, chest out posture the drill sergeants had in basic training. All wore camouflage uniforms and maroon berets (which would later be switched to black). It all intimidated me a little. These guys were a cut above. They were alpha males. Would I make the cut? I walked into the orderly room. I knew it by its distinct signs. Inside, the company clerk looked up at me. He was clean-cut and appeared to be a very professional type.

"I'd like to apply to be in your unit," I said

"What's your experience?" The company clerk said as he reached into a drawer and handed me a form to fill out.

"This is my second tour. I was here with the 25th for part of the Tet Offensive."

The clerk seemed like a friendly fellow. We spoke for a short time as he went over my paperwork. Then he looked at me intently.

"Come back tomorrow at 1300 to see the captain. Now listen to me. He's going to interview you and he's probably going to ask you what you would do if you were on a mission and you saw five NVA soldiers with an officer carrying a satchel full of documents. Answer that you would observe them carefully and report back with all the details. Do not say you would open fire on them."

"I'll remember to say that. Thanks." I thanked him, turned, and walked out.

The next day I picked through my duffel bag and put on the most presentable uniform I could prepare and went to meet with the Ranger captain. The clerk ushered me in, announced me, and sent me directly back to see him. I walked in sharply, stomped my boots together, and gave my best salute. "Sir, Specialist Grzesik reporting."

"Sit down." He motioned me to a seat. "So ... you want to join us?"

"Yes sir."

"Tell me about yourself."

I conversed with Capt. Richard Chamberlain for the better part of twenty minutes. His eyes always fixed on me as a stare. He conveyed little warmth though occasionally he smiled hard, sarcastic smiles. My overall impression of the interview was that it was going well.

He asked me about my first tour and I told him of my experience in combat and some of the situations I'd found myself in. I could tell he was reading between the lines of my answers and this allowed me to tailor my replies better. Then he popped the question the clerk warned me about. I answered that I would try to remember every smallest detail of any enemy troops I saw and that I would never open fire unless I was given the order. By the end of our meeting, I could tell he approved of me. I knew I was going to be accepted. When the meeting was over I felt a new spring in my step. Unlike some of the miserable experiences I had in the infantry where I was used as an expendable new guy, the guys I met warmed up to me easily. I already had the beginnings of great respect for them and my new unit.

Two days later, I finished the in-country orientation classes and reported to F Company Rangers permanently. I felt reborn. I felt great. I was assigned to the second platoon and most of the guys accepted me from the first day. The supply sergeant issued me camouflage fatigues and a maroon beret. But for the experience, I was now an Army Ranger.

Several days passed. During that time I was indoctrinated with the Ranger rules for operating in the jungle. We discussed patrolling, methods of tracking, listening for the enemy, and how to recognize signs he'd been there. Three days later I went on my first mission.

My heart pounded the entire morning. There was no escaping the fact that I'd gone to such great lengths to get out of going on combat missions in the infantry and yet here I was going on missions that were much more dangerous. Most concerning to me was my performance on the mission. I had to measure up to these guys. I could not fail. I had to live with myself.

I arranged my backpack first. I put a Claymore mine in it, a gallon of water, a minimal amount of hand-selected food, insect repellent, and a few other odds and ends. Sliding the supporting web gear harness over my torso, I adjusted it to fit. Then I spent some time positioning and repositioning hand grenades, a smoke grenade, a combat bandage, and two canteens of water. The last thing I did was tie a bandolier of seven magazines of ammunition over all of this. I threw three more into the backpack. When I was done I put all the stuff on and walked around for a while. It was heavy but it felt comfortable, after all, I'd done this before. An hour later we had our briefing. We were shown the objective on a chalkboard. A route was plotted out for us, an extraction point was selected and it was almost time to go.

Just before the truck picked us up to take us out to the flight-line, I applied camouflage makeup, something I had not done since basic training, and a head bandanna to keep sweat out of my eyes. The guys had been watching me unobtrusively and from a distance but no one said anything so I figured they approved of my methodology in getting ready. Out of the corner of my eye, I noticed one guy who wasn't on our team eyeing me dourly. He approached me. I did not know him, nor had I spoken to him before.

"I see you got your grenades all over the front to your web gear. That's infantry doggie style. We don't do that here in the Rangers. Put that stuff in your pack."

I did not reply, but I quickly scanned the faces of my team members for reaction. Something told me they had no opinion on the matter and would not involve themselves in it. I simply ignored the guy. I didn't know if this was a test but I made the decision right there to stand my ground. My heart sank at the thought of conflict so soon, but it never materialized.

"If you have a problem with anything I'm telling you, you can see me later." He said it coldly and left with a scowl on his face. My grenades stayed on the front of my web gear but I felt I would have a confrontation with this man in the future.

A three-quarter-ton pickup truck pulled up for us to load into. We climbed into the back of it. There was hardly any room to stand or sit because of all the equipment we had piled into it. The last person to get in, to my surprise, was my new platoon sergeant. (He would go on to be in the Ranger Hall of Fame). We rode off towards the flight line bumping and swaying with every rut we hit.

We stopped and unloaded our stuff by a Huey helicopter. The crew sat in the bird but they had not started its engine yet. Our team leader and platoon sergeant conferred with the pilots while the rest us stood around and made idle chatter. Still engrossed in my new situation, I went over every possible mission scenario. I kept checking my gear as well.

My platoon sergeant approached me. A faint smile came to his lips. "Whatcha got there?" He asked as he pointed to my hip. I followed the line of sight from his finger to my back pocket. My maroon beret was prominently sticking out of its flap. This on a sterile mission where we didn't even have identifying nametags or markings. I was mortified and managed to stammer, "I forgot that was there. Can you hold it for me?" With a grin, he nodded, took the beret, and stuck it in his own back pocket.

The pilot started the engine of the helicopter and soon the whine of the engine increased in intensity to a loud roar as rotors beat the air with that distinct Huey helicopter sound I'd heard so many times before. We climbed in and soon were airborne. As Cu Chi dropped away from us and our airspeed increased, the towns and hamlets disappeared and soon we were flying over miles of unbroken jungle. I looked around at the men and they all had the same expression. Each of them was lost in thought. Soon we would be landing in a very dangerous situation. There was nothing else to do but contemplate that fact. During the flight I got lost in thought staring at the greenery below me. In my reflection, I thought about home, my rash decision to come to Vietnam again, and what might be lurking in the jungles below me.

We flew that way for twenty minutes, quiet and introspective. Our platoon sergeant communicated with the pilots through a headset. Finally, he turned and signaled us with his hand that we were going in. The sound of the motor and the feel of the helicopter changed as we descended. Guys positioned themselves as close to the doors as possible. I'd done this before in the infantry and I chose to limit the weight of the backpack by letting it rest on the floor. I would use my torso and legs while still horizontal on the floor. Every millisecond counted once the bird touched down.

Below us, a clearing in the jungle showed light green against the much darker green of the trees around it. We would be landing there. The rough circle of the clearing got larger and larger as we descended. Soon we were upon it and before I was even aware of it, it was time to get out of the helicopter. We poured onto the landing zone from the left side of the bird and immediately raced towards the wood-line. Once there, everyone knelt facing outward while the team leader performed radio checks. The helicopter was gone and stillness descended on us and our surroundings. The first thing I noticed was the dry grass around us. I could smell it. It had been flattened by other boots. As we knelt there the heat increased by ten degrees. We hadn't been there a minute yet and I was beginning to sweat. Looking around my surroundings I was hit by the brutal reality of what I had done by coming back here. I was young and I lived by impulsive decisions. If this got too bad, I'd have to make more impulsive decisions.

When the radio check was finished we quickly moved into the wood-line. I kept craning my head to look forward. No one had to tell me to walk carefully. I had the gut feeling that I knew more about what was in this jungle than these guys did. I stepped tentatively, feeling uneasy that we were this far out in the jungle by ourselves. In the infantry, I had

Taking off on a five-day reconnaissance mission (I am second from right).

scores of armed men with me most of the time. Even on small missions we usually had a minimum of a platoon. There were only six of us and we would be traversing this jungle for five days and nights.

We'd walk a while and then stop to listen. No one ever spoke unless they had to. All communication was done in whispers. At night we'd find the thickest stuff to hide in and take turns sleeping. It continued that way for days until finally, after the fifth day, we walked into another clearing and got extracted by helicopter.

Most future missions would be similar to this one, and for the next six months, I never got shot at because the enemy never saw me though I occasionally saw him. That type of outcome was considered a perfectly executed Ranger mission because our job was to locate the enemy without him knowing we had been there.

17

Lizard

Walking in the jungle again. Six men, designated Ranger and brassy enough to have volunteered for this madness ... these walks in the jungle. That's all most Ranger missions were: slow walks in the jungle.

Our insertions into the jungle were carefully orchestrated affairs. Command and control, our radio relay station, a Cobra attack helicopter escort sometimes: all worked together during this time. Often our helicopter would make several false landings to confuse any potential enemy troops as to which landing was the real drop-off. We'd scurry into the cover of the wood-line and sit listening for any sound, hoping that the enemy was not close enough to hit us. Listening, listening, all eyes tense and seeking assurance from other silent faces; we'd sit there and hope we heard nothing. Insertion was an unpredictable, vulnerable time. Landing amid the enemy was an uncommon nightmare, but it happened occasionally and men died.

After performing radio checks and making sure we were alone, we'd walk away quickly. Insertion and extraction were the vulnerable parts of these missions. For me, leaving the insertion site felt like an escape: an escape from the eyes of an enemy we would soon attempt to find. A small army could be heading towards that spot we were leaving if they'd heard us land. We had to get away from it quickly. The jungle felt good. It hid us. Then the team leader would check his map and we'd start walking again. At the team leader's discretion, we'd stop again to listen. Walk, stop, listen. This was the method used on most of the reconnaissance missions I went on.

It was on one such mission that I had an encounter with a monitor lizard. We'd stopped for a listening break. The jungle was silent. Thick air settled upon us as we settled on the jungle floor. We sat there as still as possible. Sweat streamed down our painted, camouflaged faces. Almost frozen motionless, we blended into our surroundings. Like the jungle creatures around us, we were almost invisible. Motionless, silent, listening.

He was five feet long. He crept out from under nondescript twigs and leaves eight feet away from me. I saw him out of the corner of my eye before I had the nerve to slowly, ever so slowly, turn my head to look at him. His blackish-brown color blended almost perfectly with the jungle floor. The biggest lizard I'd ever seen in my life walked straight towards me. Four clawed, muscular legs moved in perfect symmetry, two at a time. Six inches of tongue shot out of his mouth smelling the air. He continued walking towards me. I wanted to say something to one of the guys but silence was the rule and I had a feeling this lizard might not react well to being startled.

His feet and body made a barely audible sliding, crunching sound as I sat cross-legged and frozen. He was now three feet away from me, approaching my left knee. Perhaps he knew I was there. Surely he could smell me with that radar-like tongue. Perhaps he didn't care as long as I didn't move. I sat as motionless as I could. I had seen nature shows about monitor lizards and I knew they were dangerous. Monitor lizards are not poisonous but their saliva contains pathogens and numerous bacteria. Their bite can cause an infection that results in gangrene. Medical treatment for infected monitor lizard bites is difficult at best.

His face was now two feet from my left knee. He ignored me and began digging furiously. I watched fascinated and spellbound as the primitive reptile scraped the ground with his claws. In a cat-like fashion, paw after paw, he dug approximately nine inches down. Dirt flew backward and he eventually pulled out the prize he'd been digging for. His clawed arms pulled out a perfectly round ball of animal dung. He set it down and carefully pried it in half. Inside was a teeming mass of maggots or worms. He ate them all and left the way he came. None of my teammates ever noticed.

18

M79

The M79 grenade launcher fires an explosive projectile the size of an egg up to 400 yards. We all considered it a cool weapon. Its stubby shotgun shape was unique and most guys enjoyed the unusual effect of the explosion several seconds after it was fired: a flash followed by a crunching boom. I had always wanted to carry one, so for a while, I took one out on missions. While I was in the infantry, I watched and learned the trick of launching two rounds to the same area and making them explode almost simultaneously. I did it on missions with the Rangers. I'd fire the first round in a high arc by pointing the weapon almost straight up but angled towards the target (like a mortar tube) and then quickly reload to fire the second one ... boom boom. The guys liked watching the double explosion, and I also got a big kick out of it. There was also the added bonus of the enemy not knowing the target till the two rounds exploded. In theory, this automatically doubled the firepower of the M79.

We were finishing up a mission somewhere near the Cambodian border. As usual, our team leader called for our extraction helicopter and it picked us up in a clearing. As we flew away a sniper took a shot at us. We all heard the distinct crack of his rifle. It sounded like the snap of popcorn popping next to one's ear. Sitting squarely in the doorway, I reacted quickly and fired my M79 in the direction I thought the sound came from though there was no way of telling for sure. We'd been warned before about firing out of aircraft and I found out why that day. The pilot had banked the aircraft to turn and go back to base in the direction he had come from. When he did this the aircraft attitude changed (i.e., the aircraft was tilted in relation to the horizon). For various reasons including centrifugal force, I was not aware of this.

I watched the grenade fly, at 267 feet per second, right between our helicopter's rotors. This was my first misadventure with an M79 and only a few missions later, I had another one that was just as unnerving.

The gray gloom of the jungle had lightened. Soon, spangles of light penetrated the thinning trees. They splashed randomly on the jungle floor illuminating us and our surroundings enough for caution to set in. Our pace slowed. Through the diminishing foliage, we could see the clearing that was our extraction point. Our team leader got on the radio as we stopped to scout the landing zone and the wood-line beyond it for signs of anything out of the ordinary. He was brand new in-country. He stood out as a fresh-faced sergeant newly out of non-commissioned officer school. He also was a Ranger school graduate and was as amiable a team leader as one could ask for.

We'd been in the jungle for five days. The mission had been uneventful and a helicopter was on its way to pick us up. Our job, at this point, was to secure the LZ so the bird could safely extract us. All too often the enemy waited in ambush at these LZ's during insertions or extractions.

Sometimes they planted booby traps. On the team leader's command, we walked out into the center of the LZ. We strode briskly but quietly with weapons at the ready for his order to fire. Preparing, or "prepping" the LZ involved laying down a barrage of fire in all directions to minimize the possibility of attack during the helicopter's descent. He approached me.

"The bird's coming in from there," he said, pointing.

"Don't fire past that area." He pointed further to the right.

"Got it," I said.

I'd been carrying an M79 grenade launcher for the last few missions and I'd gotten pretty good with it. The newness of carrying one of our cooler weapons was beginning to wear off. Too many times during our missions I had come to the uncomfortable conclusion that the vegetation around us was too thick to fire explosive projectiles. This effectively rendered my M79 useless in those situations. I could even injure my own men if I used it. I had already decided that I was going back to an M16 rifle soon.

I flicked the safety off of my '79 and looked where our new team leader had pointed. Then I added a twenty-degree safety margin that put me thirty yards to the left of the spot. In my line of sight stood a solitary, giant tree. I scanned the top of the huge, hundred-foot, triple canopy tree. A flowering spread of green branches sat on the top of its massive trunk. I fantasized that a tallow-skinned sniper could be sitting in those branches, waiting to shoot down my helicopter. I aimed at the center of the top of the tree. As the helicopter came in the team leader gave the order to fire. I squeezed the trigger of my M79.

The explosive projectile streaked out of my weapon and exploded in the center of the top of the tree. At the same time, our helicopter appeared from behind that tree. If I'd missed the tree several feet to the left, I might have shot down my own helicopter, possibly ablaze in aviation fuel. The round might have gone in one door and out the other missing the bird entirely.

My team leader always chided me about that day. He liked to say, "If you'd have shot down my extraction bird, I'd have kicked your ass and made you walk back to Cu Chi." Though we both chose to see the humor in that incident, we knew how close to tragedy we'd come.

19

SKS Rifle

We've all heard the expression "Angel on my shoulder" or the query "What are the odds of that happening." Though I was brought up in the strict Catholic traditions, I was always more guided by the scientific and logical. I will open this story by asking the reader: What are the odds of that happening? I read somewhere that the SKS rifle is the cockroach of military rifles but I digress....

Between reconnaissance missions, most of us had time to spend just sitting around the barracks back at Cu Chi, catching up on sleep or writing letters. In the gloom of my black and gold painted wooden hooch, I flipped an enemy round from hand to hand. It was a 7.62mm × 39: the standard AK47 round that also fit other enemy weapons. Every one I'd ever looked at seemed to have a dull brown casing instead of a shiny brass one as our ammo did. The actual bullet in it seemed more coppery, a deeper red metal than our full metal jacket ammo. Palm out in front of me, I stared at the round in my hand. As I continued flipping the bullet from hand to hand, I wondered what the powder was like compared to ours. I decided to find out.

Exiting the dark hooch into the brilliant Vietnamese sunlight, I crossed our compound to the supply sergeant's hooch and borrowed a pair of pliers from him. Then I went back to my hooch and loosened the bullet by alternately rotating and pressing it into a piece of 2 × 4 wood till it became loose enough to extract with the pliers. I poured the powder out onto the ground. It consisted of tiny rods instead of the round flakes of powder I'd seen in M16 bullets I'd taken apart. I reassembled the cartridge with great care afterward and put it in my pocket. For all intents and purposes, the round looked just as it had before but it was now devoid of powder.

Two months passed. One day, in between missions, I was approached by one of my buddies from another platoon. They had made a couple of kills and brought back some enemy equipment.

"Hey man, what's going on?" he greeted me.

"Nothin' much, I just got back from a mission yesterday. You just coming in?" I replied.

"Yeah, we did an ambush and I brought back an SKS rifle. You want it, because I don't. It's a piece of crap," he said.

"Hell yeah, I'll take it," I replied, thrilled to have an enemy war souvenir.

I took the rifle back to my hooch and set it by my bunk. I'd play with it now and again. I'd hold it up to my shoulder and look through the sights. I usually worked the action back and forth and pulled the trigger. It seemed to be a weapon in perfect operating condition. After all, it was taken from a soldier in combat. One day, as I was going through my stuff I found that loose AK47 round. As I held it in my fingers I looked down at the SKS rifle. I'd never tried loading a bullet in it before. It fired 7.62mm × 39's just like the one I was holding. I picked the rifle up with my left hand and pulled the bolt back with my right, still holding the round. I held the charging lever back carefully with my left thumb and inserted the round directly into the open chamber in front of the bolt. I seated it as well as I could and released the charging lever to see how smoothly the bullet would load.

The bolt shot forward and as it pushed the back of the round, I heard the distinct snap of the primer in the back of the round going off, though the bolt had not yet fully closed. The weapon had malfunctioned catastrophically. In normal operation, nothing should touch a primer except the firing pin when the trigger is pulled.

I'd forgotten that I'd emptied that round of powder. Had I not done so, the primer would have ignited it and exploded the brass casing, sending fragments towards my face, possibly injuring or blinding me.

20

Most Embarrassing Moment

I didn't like the splashing, sloshing sound my boots were making. Seven pairs of jungle boots all made that sound as we slogged through the jungle. We could probably be heard further away than we could see.

It had started raining heavily in one of the provinces north of the area we were operating in but that information had not been factored into our mission when we were briefed. By the third day, we had water up to our knees and rising. The team leader kept referencing his map but nothing made sense to him. Towards afternoon, water lapped at the gear around my waist and some of my ammunition was beginning to get submerged. Ammo was designed to be water-resistant but not water-proof. The thought bothered me.

We moved through waist-deep water in slow motion. After a while, we tried reversing our direction to where we came from yet the water got deeper still. The heavy rains in the north had overflowed the river. We were patrolling a flooded jungle with rising water. When all options were exhausted, Tom, our team leader, called for an extraction heli-copter. We no longer had a viable mission and depending on the extent of the flooding, the possibility of his team drowning influenced his decision.

I looked around and wondered how we could board a helicopter in our situation. Glancing around, I could see that the space between trees was tight. A bird could make it in, but just barely. Then the pilot would have to hover over water. The whole thing looked too tricky to attempt.

Our team leader had been on the radio for a few minutes now and it was clear he had been having problems solving our dilemma. He looked up at us urgently and said, "A bird is on the way to pick us up and get us out of here. Neel, pop a smoke."

We Had to Get Out of That Place

Our machine gunner, Neel, slid his pack off deftly, undid the straps, and reached in to grab a smoke grenade. He put his pack back on quickly and looked around. I could tell he didn't know where he was going to detonate the grenade. Water had blanketed the entire jungle around us. Suddenly, we heard the beat of approaching helicopter rotors. With a blank look on his face, Neal pulled the pin and threw the smoke grenade. The primer popped audibly as the smoke grenade arced up into the air and then splashed into three feet of water. A few seconds passed and with a gurgling sound, we saw purple bubbles where we should have had a plume of purple smoke. Meanwhile, the sound of the approaching bird got louder and louder. I put my weapon on a fallen tree trunk protruding from the water and quickly pulled another smoke grenade from my gear. I always carried one on the outside. With my left hand, I pulled the pin, let the spoon (handle) fly, and waited for the grenade to go off in my hand. I'd have a few seconds before it got hot. My hand jerked as it popped. A second later thick purple smoke billowed out of it and I set it on the same log my rifle sat on. The pilot confirmed the smoke color with the team leader before the bird came in. Then, it slid into view and hovered over us lowering a jungle penetrator which came down right where I was standing. It almost hit my head so I grabbed it, opened it up, and straddled it. With a smug sense of satisfaction, I thought about how I had shown the guys how to pop smoke under waterlogged conditions, and how to go up on a jungle penetrator. The winch operator on the bird began hoisting me up. As I rode up towards the bird I looked down.

I'd left my weapon behind. It was still on the log near the spent smoke grenade.

21

Large, Small Men

One never knows the nature of a man until he has been tested and his truth is revealed to all. It is not enough to reveal it to one or two people because a facade can easily resurrect itself. The truth must be revealed to all for it to be seen clearly and remembered. Only then can the facade be broken forever. The truth can crush a man but it can also build him ... but quantifying and definitions don't really matter because anything other than the truth needs no affirmation.

Men were often tested in hard units like the Ranger company I was in. Small, long-range units, and the personnel in them, had to have uncompromised character and reliability. If there was any doubt about a man, he was confronted or even challenged. Situations were usually worked out by simply bringing things out into the open. Sometimes, men just couldn't see eye to eye and altercations followed. Often these altercations were encouraged to clear the air and establish a hierarchy. After all, we were all predators.

In my four months of going out on these Ranger missions, nothing had changed. We got briefed before the mission and given whatever intel was available at the time. Then we'd go out on another mission and try to gather more intel. We were almost always delivered by helicopter and taken out the same way.

I now carry the aid bag. I have been on more than ten of these reconnaissance missions and have had the ongoing luck of never having being shot at. Though this is fortunate, it makes me very nervous. The very purpose of our missions is to find the enemy. The odds are, one day they will see us first, and if they do, they will try to kill us. Firefights by their very nature, are dangerous but they are often deadly to small units like ours operating on long-range missions where reinforcement can take time.

It's late afternoon and we're walking quietly, as usual. I constantly peer ahead and to the sides. We stop once in a while and listen carefully to our surroundings. As we walk, we observe the vegetation for indications of any previous enemy presence. Breaks in branches, flattened torn grass or an unusually quiet jungle are just a few of the signs we look for. I once even saw a man put his ear to the ground but I found it too cowboys-and-Indians to be credible. On one of our listening stops our team leader sends me out laterally, with another man, to recon a hundred yards to our 3 o'clock. I have done this before on other missions and I completely disagree with this tactic. I think it is extremely dangerous, serves little purpose, and can easily give our position away. Once, we got lost and had to fire a shot into the dirt to get a return shot to regain our bearing. I considered that severely compromising to the mission.

It is late afternoon when we walk up to a clearing. Just inside the wood-line, before the clearing, is a series of old foxholes similar to the ones I saw in Dau Tieng two years earlier. Our team leader decides to stop here for the night though it is still light. I assume that he wants to observe the clearing and be able to use the foxholes as defensive positions even though they are very small. The average North Vietnamese soldier or Vietcong is around a hundred and twenty-five pounds. We can fit into those holes, but just barely. The clearing itself is less than 100 yards across. High grass grows across most of it but we can see to the other side if we sit up.

The afternoon passes into the evening quietly. We have our meals and prepare for the night. When I put out my Claymore mine I realize its range will be very limited because of the grass. Day turns to dusk and then dark as my guys prepare to take turns sleeping.

Around 1 a.m. (0100), as my eyes peer through the darkness with its usual phantasms and imaginings, I see a bright light directly across the clearing from me. I quickly but very silently waken the rest of the team. We all stare at the light as it flashes towards us, then away and back. I can't tell if he's looking for us or trying to signal us. Either way, it doesn't matter. There are no friendlies out here and my instinct tells me we have been detected. My heart pounds as I ready my gear for combat. Every movement seems ten times louder than it actually is. Everyone is rustling in preparation. The sound is maddening though I understand it is not as loud as I think it is. Then I heard it.

"Mamma, Mamma." One of our guys, the same one who threatened me for not wearing my equipment to his liking, is curled up on the ground like a baby moaning and crying for his mother. I cannot believe it. To me, this behavior is chicken shit and almost beyond comprehension. Not a shot has been fired at us and we don't know for sure that the enemy has even seen us, yet this tough guy has broken down into a useless, blubbering pile.

I crawl over to him and hiss into his ear. "If you make another sound I'll kill you myself. Just stay here and shut your mouth."

He looked up at me with frightened but understanding eyes and nodded his head. By now our team leader is on the radio. I could hear him giving our grid coordinates with his coded book. Meanwhile, the light kept sweeping in our direction. Then it went out. Less than a minute later I heard the beautiful sound of incoming artillery. I expected the sound of thunderous explosions and instead illumination flares popped over the clearing. I was surprised and a little dismayed that the team leader had called for illumination. In my opinion, this did nothing but give away our position and verify the fact that we were there. To this day I believe we spent the rest of the night in twice as much danger. I believe he should have called in high explosives to blow the other side of the clearing to bits. While all this was going on he got a message over the radio that there was a company of NVA soldiers in our area and that the light probably belonged to them.

I never spoke to the coward tough guy again and he avoided me for the rest of my time in the Rangers. Only a month passed before I had another encounter with another tough guy. This one was not a coward but a bully. It was late in the afternoon. The sky had turned a slate gray and soon that twilight would fade to black. I was walking near the back of our compound towards our little clubhouse when he stepped out of the shadows. I would've never noticed him and just kept walking but for the malicious, almost angry stare on his face. I hardly knew the guy but in an instant, I knew I was in trouble. This man had a meanness and hostility about him that would not be denied. I'd walked into the wrong spot at the wrong time. I'm sure that if it had not been me it would have been someone else ... but it was me.

By my own standards, I was never a tough kid. The tough guys in New York were obvious. They hung out on street corners well past the curfew times other teens had. They usually had well-greased hair. Some wore leather jackets with upturned collars. Their distinct posture conveyed a deliberate and intended tone of menace. They bore an exaggerated body language that warned off the weaker of us till we paid sufficient homage. Despite their admonitory persona, they could be befriended if the correct balance of deference and respect was rendered. We'd stand in quiet semicircles and listen to their stories of weight lifting, fistfights, run-ins with the law, and sexual conquests and they usually didn't mess with us. Often, they stuck up for us against bullies. I'd never met a bully in the Army before.

He looked to be over two hundred pounds and I could tell by his steps, plodding and heavy, that he was drunk. I tried to turn around to leave quickly but was immediately corralled by several of his redneck friends. One shoved me back towards him. I had no idea why this was happening though I'd seen it happen before, growing up in New York. I turned back to face my would-be tormentor. He slogged directly towards me and his face now had the added quality of amusement. He knew I couldn't get away. I knew it too and accepted my fate. I assumed a boxing position and we both went around in a circle like fighters in a ring. It was then that I realized he was barefoot. Till now I had kept control by going around him in repeated circles. He could not step as quickly and easily as I because of his drunkenness and bare feet. Also, he appeared to be getting dizzy. I seized the opportunity because the timing seemed perfect. I jumped in and stomped on one of his feet with all my might. I jumped back just as quickly. He shuddered and limped two steps with a look of total surprise. Before he could recover, I jumped back in and stomped the other foot. He could barely stand now so I did a flying tackle grabbing him around his neck in a headlock. We landed in a heap beside a Jeep and I dragged him under it, slowly but surely, as I punched his face repeatedly. I looked up again and again, fearing someone in his group would attack me but no one did. I wound up beating the hell out of the guy. I would have stopped hitting him earlier but I very much believed I had to put him down hard or he might still get me.

The next morning I sat on the edge of our perimeter scared of what the day might bring. The guy I'd beaten in a drunken state was now sober, hungover, and sore. If he came for me again, I feared I would not fare as well. I sat on the sandbags by the edge of our camp contemplating this when one of my guys came up to me and said, "Grzesik, I don't think you have anything to worry about. That guy you beat the shit out of woke up this morning, looked in the mirror, and said, 'I don't know who did this to me but I must've deserved it.'"

22

A Beautiful Jungle

No two missions were ever the same. Some were fraught with danger while others played out simply as long walks in the woods. Weather, terrain, physical exertion ... many elements shaped a mission and often the strong but diverse personalities of our guys lent missions their most vibrant characteristics. Sometimes when a confluence of personalities, events, and environment had just the right makeup, it made for memorable missions without anything remarkable taking place.

We received intel that the enemy was infiltrating an area bordered by a river. There was some reason to believe they had built an underwater crossing. I played with the thought and couldn't conceive how or why anyone would need an underwater bridge. I conjured thoughts of rocks piled under the water but I had seen few rocks, if any, in my time in Vietnam. Certainly, any type of platform would require ropes on either side and would be visible but we had to work with the intel we got, and I was on the team chosen to recon the area.

I met the guys I was going out with outside the briefing room. At a glance, it appeared we'd all been selected from different teams. Conversation flowed easily. We all knew each other by name and my intuition told me that we would get along well. We could not have had a more compatible group. My feeling was this was going to be a laid-back mission, but I could not have asked for a better group if we did make contact with the enemy. The briefing was more interesting than most. We would insert by helicopter some distance from the actual area to be reconnoitered, and then climb a hill overlooking it. Our objective was the river.

Most of my experience with the Rangers had been in flat, mostly jungle-covered terrain. At my 149 lbs, there were limitations to the weight I could carry. My rucksack had already been trimmed to the bare minimum and I was concerned about being able to climb with it. The thought of slowing a team down concerned me. It always had.

We Had to Get Out of That Place

I suited up, hopped a truck with the others to the flight-line, and we took off. As usual, even a long flight ended way too quickly and soon we saw the hills we would land among below us. They reminded me of North Carolina from the air. Shortly after that, we descended. The pilot took the bird down between trees and just before we touched down, rose abruptly. He did this again two hundred meters later. The third landing, in a clearing the size of a house plot, was the actual one. The others had been ruses to confuse the enemy.

We ran to the close-by wood-line and hid twenty meters behind it till we felt sure no one was coming toward us. We began walking: slowly at first to be sure our arrival was undetected, then after several hundred meters, we picked up the pace. Sweat streamed down my forehead into my headband. The hottest part of the day had settled upon us heavily and we kept walking, stopping only for listening breaks and drinks of water. As we walked, the vegetation around us got thinner, though it appeared more luxurious. It allowed for easier walking. The hues of the jungle seemed to get darker as well: a deeper richer green. We took another break.

As we sat there, alert and listening, a palpable serenity befell us. Muted jungle sounds in the distance mixed with our whispers. Men smiled when they spoke. My instincts told me we were totally alone out here. We sat there longer than we should have, simply enjoying the moment: we didn't care. I wondered if it was just me appreciating our surroundings, and as I looked at the guys again, I realized that most of them were as enthralled and beguiled by the beauty before them as I. It almost felt as if we were taking in some grand view in a national park, but it was only the natural beauty of the jungle. The sunlight here came in wisps of chiffon and sharp daggers. Bright emerald leaves the size of doors blazed on sparkling jade backgrounds as the verdant palette retreated to forest greens and the black behind them. I'd been in jungle this pretty before while marching with the infantry, but those were sterner times when I served with men rigid and cold in the danger that was their business. These Rangers I served with now had the luxuries of moving fast and being able to smile in adversity. They were a far cry from the sullen draftees who slogged with downward gazes through the mud and counted their days. The trade-off of the predictable for the unknown had its consequences, however. Some Ranger teams were never heard from again after being inserted.

We walked till the evening and set up for the night in a patch of thicker vegetation. That night we slept well. Hidden in our thicket, with Claymore mines surrounding us, we felt secure taking turns on guard duty while the others slept. Peaceful muted sounds of the sleeping jungle lulled me into a restful slumber when my time on watch was over.

We walked again the next day and the day after that. But for the weight we carried and the ever-present possibility of the enemy, our journey was a pleasant one. It was in fact the most scenic Ranger mission I'd ever been on. On the fourth day, we walked onto a slight incline that gradually became a slope. We weren't walking up an actual hill, just a steady sloping grade. Though more tiring than flat jungle, our march was not at all difficult.

We slowed our ascent as we approached the top of the grade. Our objective was somewhere near the top of our climb. Vegetation was sparser now and I could see the top of the ridge several hundred yards away. By the time we approached it we were all sweating and panting. Near the top, we moved carefully, trying to stay hidden in whatever cover there was. Finally, we saw the crest of the hill. The other side of the hill dropped more abruptly than the side we had come up on. Below it wound the S-shaped ribbon that was the river. We stared at it fascinated but it was evening and soon we retreated to thicker vegetation to set up for the night. Then, in the morning we carefully walked back to the top and set up a vantage point where we could observe the river while hidden in the brush. The day passed quickly. We sat there and watched the river and its banks till late afternoon. Because of our camouflage, we probably couldn't be seen by anyone, but any movement could have given us away if anyone scanned the ridge. We could observe the furthest end of the river, about a thousand yards away, and the closest end just below us, about two hundred yards. We sat there silently for hours and the only sound was our murmured conversations or the rustle of our gear. The river made no sound. Not a wisp of air moved and the surrounding forest seemed unnaturally quiet. I turned to a teammate.

"You notice how quiet it is?"

"Yeah, I was thinking about that."

"I don't like it when it's too quiet."

"Me neither, it sounds suspicious." He grinned at me.

Our team leader overheard us and chuckled softly. Later, when he made one of his situation reports over the radio, he mentioned the quiet. When he was done he looked up at us.

"Guys, they're sending out the Vietnamese Air Force."

"What in the hell for?" someone asked.

"I think they want to drop some ordnance. All I did was say it seemed too quiet."

"Jesus Christ," another voice exclaimed.

Five minutes later, from the far end of the river, we heard the approach of the planes. They came in low over the river, and within seconds began dropping their bombs. The flash of the explosions followed by their shockwaves sent us all scrambling to put the top of the ridge between us and the blasts. Our team leader stayed on the radio as we all looked at each other wide-eyed. "We need to get back down to the bottom of the hill. An armored unit is coming to pick us up," he said.

We ran back the way we came. I couldn't understand the logic of what was going on and my only concern was the blast radius of the bombs being dropped. When we got to our rendezvous point, only minutes passed before the column of tanks and armored personnel carriers (APCs) arrived.

We were told to get into an APC for our safety and it drove away with us inside. I'd always hated the thought of armor. The din of the motors and the clanking of the tracks could be heard far away. The dust plumes they made were visible for miles. The worst part for me was that one enemy soldier could kill a tank or carrier and all its occupants with an RPG rocket. For five days, we'd walked all-seeing but unseen and now we could see nothing, yet our presence was known to everyone.

We rode in that carrier for fifteen minutes struggling to breathe in its heat and fumes when they let us out to ride on top. As we rode, their gunners fired into the surrounding tall grass and trees. I couldn't wait for it to be over, because I felt we could get hit at any time.

We eventually got picked up by helicopter and were back in Cu Chi an hour later. During our debriefing, we had literally nothing to report. We would have asked why the airstrike was ordered but the answer might have required more questions.

23

Cambodia

I was in between missions and just relaxing in my hooch when I heard them. Multiple authoritative voices boomed through the company area. Something was up so I got up to see what was going on. As I poked my head through the entryway, I saw my platoon sergeant about to come in.

"Everybody. Right now. Heavy mission with a double basic load. Company formation in fifteen minutes." He turned to leave.

"Where are we going?" I asked.

He turned back around and waited a second before he answered, as though he might be betraying a confidence. "We might be going to Cambodia to evacuate the U.S. Embassy."

I simply stared at him. He stared back at me and there was no mistaking the urgency in his eyes. Then he turned and left without another word.

Just like that, with almost no warning, I was on a mission. Adrenaline supercharged my body and I was instantly in a race to not be grouped with the last guys to be ready. My first thought turned to my gear. I immediately regretted not having it ready. Usually, after a mission, we just dumped our stuff and worked on it later. When another mission was announced, we normally had plenty of time to get everything in order. Not this time.

I sprinted out of my hooch and back around to our storage bunker where we kept our ammo and gear. In the dimness, I instinctively found my equipment. It sat neatly spaced in the row of backpacks and M16 rifles lined against the back wall. My canteens and grenades always remained on my suspender harness and belt which lay folded over my backpack. On top of that lay a bandolier of rifle ammo. I never took my gear apart. Other guys appeared behind me. Scooping everything up, I ran back to my hooch where I dumped it all on my bunk and stared at it briefly. What would I need on a mission like this? I decided against the two-quart canteen. Extracting a handful of embassy personnel should not take that long I thought as I grabbed both quart canteens on my pistol belt and filled them with water. We always had plenty of iodine water purification pills in case we had to re-fill the canteens with contaminated water. Then I went back to the ammo bunker and grabbed two more bandoliers of ammunition and four more hand grenades, for a total of four bandoliers and eight grenades. It all went into the backpack.

Everyone always said I carried too many grenades, but to me, the idea of being able to throw powerful explosions in any direction was a comfort. I picked up the Claymore mine and examined it carefully to make sure there were no breaks in the detonator wire. Though I couldn't think of a situation where I would need a Claymore, I decided to bring it anyway because it was a lethal anti-personnel weapon and I could blow a hole in the side of a building with it if I had to. I put it on the bottom of the backpack. Next into the bag went two long-range patrol meals. I took only the main meal packs out of the box and left the rest. They took very little room. After a quick lube job on my rifle, I threw the bottle of lube, along with a bottle of insect repellent, into my pack and I was done. But for applying my camouflage face paint, I was ready to go.

I looked at my watch and realized I still had time to spare so I stared at my pack and thought about what I could possibly have forgotten for going into Cambodia—a place that had been a mess since I first heard of it. Lon Nol had recently led a coup against the ruling prince, North Vietnamese troops were invading from the north, students were rioting at the embassy, Pol Pot, the communist guerrilla, scurried about the country's dense jungle preparing to commit one of the greatest genocides in history. All the while the U.S. military was bombing the country's eastern border. I wondered what in hell we even had people there for. To me, the place seemed to be in chaos and it was getting worse every day.

I imagined the hundred-mile flight to Phnom Penh. We would probably be escorted by Cobra attack helicopters. Once in place, we would secure a perimeter around the embassy while its occupants were lifted out by either Chinook or Huey helicopters. The fact that we were mustered on such short notice indicated to me that the personnel there were in trouble of some sort. Clearly, some kind of hostile element was approaching them. A simple evacuation of people would be able to be done quickly. On the other hand, if we were surrounded by a hostile force, we could be in big trouble. As I began putting my gear on, that was my final thought. If we don't get it done quickly, we could be in trouble.

The second I lifted my backpack onto my shoulder I knew I'd made a mistake, but I walked to our formation area with it on anyway. My pack weighed substantially more than it ever had before and I knew I might have a problem trying to move quickly or a long distance. Most of the company stood in place already. Our guys stood in the sun like pit bulls straining to be let go. Few of them spoke. Tension and resolve showed on all their faces. Everyone had their gear on and it was as deadly a fighting force as I had ever seen.

When our captain appeared, he said very little. He told us that hostile forces were attacking too close to the U.S. Embassy and that we would be on standby till further notice, to help get them out. He closed by simply telling us, "Be ready gentlemen."

He approached me as the formation broke up and casually asked, "What do you think of this mission?"

"If we don't get it done quickly, we could be in trouble," I replied.

We never did go to Cambodia. The danger passed. We stood down as did the aircraft crews on the runway. Cambodia and millions of its people would die in about five years, as would the Republic of Vietnam.

24

Marking Round

The mission briefing had been just another session of finger-pointing at scrawlings, circles, and squiggly marks on a chalkboard. I was beginning to think these briefings were more complicated than they needed to be. Perhaps I was getting complacent. That could get me and everyone else on my team killed. I needed to go home.

We'd be entering a certain point in the jungle and operating in the area between it and our extraction point. It was very straightforward: not a complicated issue I thought. In reality, these were complex, carefully orchestrated affairs. Everyone had to know where we were at all times, especially our reaction force, usually a fast, light infantry unit ready to fly in and support us at a moment's notice if we made contact with the enemy.

The air cover we might need was pre-arranged at the division level by people way above my pay grade. Mine was the dangerous part: go in with my team and find the enemy. I was just a young kid and knew nothing. Land, walk, don't make noise so you don't get shot, and then call a bird to get you out. My simplistic view worked well for me because of its simplicity. Looking back on it all, I don't think I ever knew where we were when out on a mission.

The pilot turned and signaled to the team leader with one finger pointed down and we all tensed. We were about to be inserted. Till now, we'd been sitting in the breeze of the bird's open cabin in silent reflection. Having been on many flights like this, even before the Rangers, I'd noticed that most men stayed silent, deep in thought, during insertion flights.

I found myself comparing the similarities in the jungle below to forest outings back home. Going for a walk with friends... My thoughts turned to what might be below us. Any thoughts of family or friends on outings faded. The warmth of those sane, warm faces blurred into the expanse of miles and circumstance as we steeled ourselves for danger. Bravado and courage were the only two useful attributes here and any welling up of emotion had to be stifled.

The whine of the helicopter's turbine lowered in pitch and we floated down onto our objective: an endless expanse of lush, billowing green jungle. Till now this place had been nothing more than several grid coordinates on a map.

The ground came up at us quickly, but just before we touched it, the pilot gunned the engines. Our bodies lurched downward with inertia as our descent suddenly stopped. The Huey stabilized and hovered a few feet off the ground. Both door gunners leaned out the door straining against their seatbelt while manning their machine guns and scanning the landing zone intensely. My team leaped out one by one. When my turn came I did a sideways twist so my pack would hit the ground at the same time my body did. I did this because at one hundred and forty-five pounds my knees could not absorb the high impact all the weight I was carrying would cause.

Thudding onto the LZ knocked some wind out of my lungs with an audible grunt. I had vague thoughts about breaking something inside the backpack or worse yet, something exploding. Warm grass pressed against my cheek as I scrambled to get off of it to right myself back to a standing position. We should have been running towards the wood line but there were multiple wood lines as the jungle was intermittent where we had been inserted. I immediately sensed confusion in the team leader by his body language. He was looking to the left and right. There was hesitation in his step. I sensed we were in trouble and I was correct. He turned, looked at us, and pointed to a piece of thicket for us to head to.

Once there we set up a small defense perimeter and he did the usual commo checks over the radio. Then he opened up his map and began studying it. This seemed odd because usually by now we'd be walking as fast as we could to get away from the insertion point and the noise our arrival had made.

"These terrain features have changed or the map is wrong," Tom said, alternating between staring at the map and looking at the landscape all around him. "We're going to take our original azimuth and see if that direction makes any sense."

He was planning to walk a kilometer or so to see if the terrain matched the map. "Let's move," he said and we began walking.

Because the vegetation we were in was sparse, much of the time we walked in sunlight. After a kilometer, my clothes were drenched. Droplets of sweat mixed with camouflage face paint rolled into my eyes and burned. At times I was temporarily blinded. It occurred to me I'd never walked in the sunlight for any length of time on a mission before. I adjusted my headband and wiped my brow trying to stop the sweat from running into my eyes. Occasionally, the unsuspected branch from the man in front of me whipped back at me. My pack's shoulder straps dug into my wet, slick jungle shirt and slipped. I'd shrug my shoulders hard to jump the pack up onto my back again. We kept moving, stopping only now and then to listen. After another kilometer, we finally stopped and set up a perimeter again. We'd walked two kilometers and had not come upon any identifiable features to correlate with the map. We were lost, but at least the terrain was getting thicker.

The team leader huddled us up again. Facing outward three hundred and sixty degrees with weapons pointed, we turned our heads and listened to him as he studied the map again.

"I'm not sure where we are. I haven't seen one damn thing I can find on the map."

"What do you want to do?" someone asked him.

He stood up, looked around, then looked back at us. "I'm going to call for a marking round."

Usually, a marking round is a projectile fired from an artillery piece. Its purpose is to create a low-level explosion on a map coordinate, near personnel, to orient them to their location relative to it. Tom knelt with the radio, selected a channel, and lifted the handset. He spoke softly into it. He'd pulled the encryption card out of his pocket and for every number of our map coordinates, he sent a scrambled series of letters over the radio to our artillery support guys. Then he looked at us. "The shot is on its way."

A 105mm projectile streaked through the sky towards us at thousands of feet per second. I couldn't help but look at the sky and imagine where it was coming from. For a fraction of a second, I heard what sounded like a whisper. Then it got very loud. SHHHHHHHHHHHH It was an ear-piercing sound: like some crazed principal silencing an auditorium of undisciplined students over the microphone.

The round hit right next to us and exploded with a loud pop, not the boom we were used to. Immediately the jungle all around us was on fire and heavy with smoke. It turned out that the coordinate that he had picked was dangerously close to the one we were sitting on. Everything around us was catching fire. We all grabbed our stuff and moved out very quickly so we wouldn't be engulfed by the flames.

We'd been right where we thought we were. We had never been lost. The jungle growth had simply changed over the years.

25

Fall from Grace
and Ascent I

Though it would last another five years, the war in Vietnam slowly crushed under its own weight and drew towards a close. We were deliberately ending a war that we were winning due to public ignorance, apathy, and the desire to save boys quite willing to fight a war. The result of this loss of, and lack of, conviction would result in the loss of millions of lives and the destruction of millions more across Southeast Asia. People didn't know it yet and wouldn't have cared anyway because patience for the war had run out. Our enemy, however, had patience. He had conviction. He had the support of his countrymen, while we did not.

In 1970, F Company Rangers downsized from four platoons to two. Sixty of us, including me, were reassigned to other units. I was awarded a medal, given a plaque, and afforded the opportunity to give a short speech bidding everyone farewell. I thanked them for allowing me the opportunity to serve in their ranks. On a sparkling clear Vietnamese day, I boarded a helicopter for my last ride out of Cu Chi. This time the destination was Tan Son Nhut Air Base in Saigon, not the jungle. From there I'd catch a plane for another journey into the unknown, but for now, I had Saigon. There would be time to party in Saigon—lots of dope, whisky, and women: the most beautiful women in the world.

For as long as I could, I would bask in the relief of not having to go out into that jungle. For a while, I would be free of the foreboding thoughts before every mission and the trip out by helicopter. Twenty times, six of us had gone out undetected. The enemy had never seen us but we'd seen them. Each time I thought that the lucky streak couldn't continue. The penny couldn't keep landing on heads, but it had. I felt that my luck had been due to run out soon.

Saigon never disappointed. I spent the night shacked up with a

Vietnamese beauty. We drank. My stupor allayed my anxiety and my youth made it easy to not think of the morrow but time passed too quickly. I had to get to Chu Lai and my new assignment before someone figured out I was taking too much time getting there. I figured I could explain a couple of days away but any more and eyebrows would raise at my new unit. I didn't want to start out on a note of disfavor or worse. On a steaming hot Saigon morning, I put on a clean uniform, checked out of my cheap hotel, and took a taxi to the main gate of Tan Son Nhut Airbase. In fifteen minutes I was on the runway waiting for a flight.

The C-7 Caribou is a large, lumbering, no-frills, Air Force plane. Unlike civilian aircraft, it has very little soundproofing, It starts with a sudden thunder. Propellers beat air and engines roar. Every moving part whines, screams, bangs, or shudders. The cacophony increases as the aircraft lifts off. Having flown on these aircraft before, I know to expect this as I sit down on the webbing and aluminum tubing that constitute a fold-down bench. I fasten my seatbelt and look around. There are many soldiers new to Vietnam on this plane. The dark green of their new uniforms and their pink faces give them away. Also obvious are the fresh haircuts and lack of weaponry. They clutch their orders tightly in their clean hands. Mine are stuffed into my pocket. New guys are easy to spot. It's going to be fun watching them as we take off.

The pilot cranks the engine and our flight begins. An aircrewman runs up and down the aisle to check seat belts. He deftly whips the cord leading to his green headphones out of his way as he reports to the pilots.

Remarkably, we are airborne fifteen minutes from the time I board the aircraft: much faster than any civilian plane I ever flew in. It only takes about three football fields of runway to get off the ground. My gaze turns to the fresh faces I was looking at earlier. They look like they're afraid we're going to crash, but after all, they are all cherries and the horrendous noise of this airplane frightens them. Where they are going is probably scarier. They will be okay once they are used to the madness that is Vietnam ... or they may die.

"You going to Chu Lai?" One of the cherries yells to me over the din of the plane.

"Yeah," I answer.

"What's it like?"

"Same as anywhere else. You guys infantry?" I evade his question with my own question.

"Yeah, all three of us are going to the Americal Division."

I look at the newbies with a pitying cold eye. I'm not going to frighten them with the truth or lull them with a lie. They don't deserve either yet. Those will come soon enough. They are flying to perdition in the jungle.

My gaze turns towards the windows of the aircraft and I can see the countryside below. I have been flying around this country for two years and the craters in the landscape still amaze me. I have never flown and not seen bomb or artillery scars in the land. I alternately nap and stare out the window.

The realization that we are floating down onto the landscape below stirs me. The motors wind to a lower sound and the landing gear thumps into the open position. We are landing in Chu Lai. Soon I will be speaking with the people who will assign me to my next duty station. The thought worries me. I have decided I'm not going out into that jungle again. I'm not doing it. I'm not going to die here.

Chu Lai spreads west from the beach on the South China Sea just south of Da Nang. It is home to the Americal Division and several helicopter units. The terrain is flat and mostly sand. Originally a Marine base, it was taken over by the Army in 1967. Though it has many of the same aspects of Cu Chi, the feel is distinctly different.

Stepping out of the door of the C7 caribou, I tread down the ramp quickly. My step is hastened by the fact that if I don't get this done correctly, I may be assigned to the infantry again. Despite the rigid standards of the Army, there was sometimes flexibility and I have to work this perfectly. Getting assigned to something other than your MOS (military occupational specialty) requires skill; somebody has to be talked into doing it for you. Ahead of me, I see a guy walking casually, gaze cast downward, wearing rumpled fatigues. Perfect—he'll be the guy to ask. He's been here so long he's bored but he knows everything.

"Hey man, you know where division headquarters is?"

"Yeah," he says as he points. "You can't miss it."

"Thanks."

The case I will plead is very simple and straightforward. What I have to do is sound convincing and articulate. It's my second tour and for six months I've been a Ranger. I deserve something better than to simply slog in the jungle with the Infantry.

I march into the Americal Division headquarters, orders in hand, and present my case to the first intake personnel I speak to. They refer me to a major. He asks me what I'd like to do and I reply, "door gunner on a helicopter." Just like that, I am assigned to the 176th Helicopter Assault Company (and later the 174th).

When I arrived at my new unit, I was welcomed and, to my amazement, offered R&R. They seemed almost eager to give me a vacation. I set up my bunk in my new tent quarters, slept there one night, and headed right back to Saigon to continue my revelry before actually checking in for R&R and more merriment.

I caught a helicopter going my way and overnight I found myself back where I'd been just several days ago. Though I still felt drawn and tired from booze, dope, and women, I was eager and ready to do it again. To a young soldier like me, Saigon's many bars, massage parlors, and opium dens presented opportunities never available back home. For war-weary troops, the pleasure and oblivion readily available here was the ultimate relief if they were lucky enough to get to visit. Saigon stood as the capital of Vietnam and the seat of power for all old wealth, but it was also its seamy underbelly. Here, heroin could be bought on any street corner yet the Presidential Palace, regal and aloof with a huge police and military presence, stood relatively close by.

On my first tour in '68, I had visited plenty of opium dens but by 1971, heroin was the drug of choice for most GIs. I needed no introduction to it. I had tried it several times before the draft ripped me from the decadence of the sixties. It was by far the best drug for the situation I was in. Smoother and deeper than cocaine, its tentacles soothed rather than ratcheted the psyche. I'd always been careful with marijuana because I was one to get paranoid reactions to it. Many guys smoked it but my mental state was still too frail from the bad LSD experience to trifle with more mind-altering drugs. Just the thought of getting that reaction in combat frightened me. To a certain extent, I even justified my heroin use. It subdued feelings of loneliness and boredom, but best of all, it subdued fear. Screaming hordes of crazed attackers from the Vikings to the Viet Cong had used drugs or alcohol to achieve the effect to steeling themselves during battle. I sometimes rationalized: if they did it, so could I.

I started with a massage at a joint near the main gate of Tan Son Nhut Airbase where I'd landed for the second time in less than a week. A pretty woman greeted me at the top of a staircase whose entrance beckoned out in the street below under a massage sign. She waved me in with a smile that suggested we both knew what I was there for. I'd never experienced erotic pleasures like these in my youth and I arrived in Vietnam as a virgin. My sexual tension was as tight as a guitar string. I disrobed and mounted a table I recognized as a piece of American hospital equipment. She covered my rear with a towel and begin working on me. Though I was young, the massage had rejuvenating effects. Too many missions, sleep deprivation, and recent partying had wreaked havoc on my body. She kneaded me with practiced fingers. At one point she took off her sandals and climbed up on the table and walked on my back. The entire time I eyed her tight, subtle curves as she made occasional eye contact. When she flipped me over to massage my front, I slid my hand over her flawless, silky skin and though she somewhat resisted, she smiled. Occasionally she'd slide her fingers across the towel over my groin while smiling slyly at me. She hinted that she could make me happy for an extra few dollars. I agreed and it only took another ten seconds for her to accomplish it spectacularly.

I bounded out of there alive and refreshed, my feet booming down three stairs at a time. Once outside, my eyes squinted to adjust to the light as I began walking. The square mile around the main gate of Tan Son Nhut afforded me everything I wanted. The hotels and bars beckoned to me. Pharmacies sold amphetamines and barbiturates legally if I wanted another high. Bustling blocks of open-air markets sold everything from toiletries to sunglasses and everything in between. Before me, the splendors of Saigon's netherworld spread out as far as I could see, like a giant buffet waiting for me to sample it. Many items in these markets were pilfered from the military supply system or the docks in Saigon. Payment could be made in Dong (South Vietnamese currency), MPC (Military Payment Certificates), or American dollars, though mere possession of these was illegal for soldiers in Vietnam.

I felt safer in this part of Saigon. In case of any type of attack, I could probably find Americans. The streets here roared with serpentine traffic towards the main base gate as well as away from it. Squealing brakes, blaring horns, and revving motors all blended into a chaotic cacophony perfumed by the smoke of burning engine oils ... and the smell, always the sweet smell that was unique to Vietnam. Cyclos, taxis, Lambrettas, and motorcycles all competed for the fastest lane they could muscle into. In an emergency situation, I could always hail one of those vehicles or run a mile to the main gate; after all, I'd done it in a little over six minutes in basic training. I always liked having my M16 rifle with me but I didn't have it on this trip because I was going on R&R.

That made me a little uneasy. After all, I was planning on spending the night in Saigon.

I had no game plan when I hit the street but my opium connection here, Kwi, was right around the corner and a few blocks down. I met her on my first tour of Vietnam when I had more freedom to travel during my time with the 36th Engineer Battalion. I headed in her direction. Whenever I made it to Saigon, my thoughts turned warm and easy to her. Knowing Kwi was like knowing a cool stoned aunt, always welcoming, always polite, and always having lots of dope: which in this case was opium. She made me feel special and I'm sure, in the ways of her ancient culture, she meant to do just that.

A few more sandal shops, a few more drug stores, and there it was. Another nondescript stairway leading up from the street. At the top of it sat Kwi's opium den. I walked up quietly because quiet was always the manner at Kwi's. I knocked softly and listened for her approach but heard nothing. Then she opened the door quietly just enough to see who I was. Her feet were bare and she wore black silk pajama bottoms and a white silk top.

"Hi!" She exclaimed "You come. Long time I no see you."

"Long time I kill VC. Long time I no can come." I grinned as she waved me in.

"You be careful. VC *caca dau* [kill] you, GI." She grinned back at me.

"Never happen," I replied.

I always had to have the last word on this subject when brought up by a Vietnamese because the alternative was to agree. The subject was uncomfortable and I always felt an odd combination of defensiveness and foreboding. These people knew more about the enemy than I did. They probably had friends who were Viet Cong sympathizers. Sometimes it felt like being in a crowd of high school students who knew who the bully was, and knew that he was coming to get you, yet they would or could say nothing.

The quiet warm and welcoming gloom of Kwi's apartment enveloped me as I stepped inside. A cloying mustiness, the result of sweet opium smoke permeating everything inside over the years, hung in the air. My boots thumped lightly as I walked in and I felt self-conscious about that. I always felt like they didn't belong in here and that I should have left them outside. Such niceties were impractical, however. I usually left a loaded M16 rifle leaning against her wall when I visited.

Two features stood out in Kwi's apartment: scattered pillows and mats on the floor near the center of the room and a shiny hardwood sleeping platform that resembled an expensive table ... one with short legs. On the end of it, by the wall, sat a headrest made of the same wood. It resembled a footstool. This was a Vietnamese bed and pillow. They would roll a mat out on this furnishing and sleep on their backs. They may have had nightclothes, I don't know. I was always grateful to get these fascinating glimpses into their alien culture.

Kwi swept her palm towards the mats and pillows on the floor. That was where we would smoke opium.

I lowered myself onto one of the mats and placed my head on a pillow. From there I watched the ritual begin. Kwi produced an opium pipe and begin preparing it. She did all this from a squatting position. Vietnamese rarely sat in chairs. Their very slight body weight allowed them to sleep or rest in positions not possible for our beefy Caucasian frame. Thus, where we would sit, Vietnamese squatted. They could do so for extended periods. Their legs, especially their knees, were acclimated to this.

The pipe itself was ornate. For all I knew, it could have been hundreds of years old. It was made of fine polished wood and carefully hammered brass. The stem was about an inch wide with brass on both ends. The bowl sat three-quarters of the way down the stem. It too was made of brass and wood and resembled a doorknob.

With practiced fingers, Kwi dipped a thin metal rod into a vial of opium gracefully and heated it with a hypnotic, twirling motion. Each time she did so the opium on the rod bubbled and got thicker. She packed this into the bowl opening. When she was done, she prepared a hole in the packed opium for flame and suction to facilitate smoking. Holding the pipe to a small coconut oil lamp, she'd take a small puff to start it properly and then let me have the rest of the bowl.

Only my fingertips handled my end of the pipe; she held the rest of it. Each inhalation felt like a ghost of pleasure, relaxation, and peace entering my soul. I lay there as the ritual repeated itself over and over with Kwi making occasional eye contact with me, all the while smiling gently. I nodded off into a warm cocoon.

"You feel good now?" I opened my eyes to see Kwi's smiling face and grinned.

"I give you five dollars, okay?" She smiled and nodded.

"Next time you come you go PX for me."

"OK, next time." Though the practice was illegal, all Vietnamese wanted soldiers to buy goods from the PX for them. They made considerable money selling these items on the black market.

I rose with some reluctance, paid Kwi, and after some small talk, walked back out into the din that was Saigon.

As I walked I thought about the last time I left Kwi's place. I had walked in this same mellow state and ambled down this same street fidgeting with a wart on my right index finger. It had bothered and offended me for years so I lifted my hand to my mouth, grabbed it with my teeth, yanked it out, and spit it into the gutter. I had pulled the entire thing out down to the root, almost to the bone. The wound was perfectly circular and precise. It didn't bleed much so I found something to wrap it with and I was done with it. A doctor could not have done a better job. Opium overcame fear, pain, and sensible inhibitions.

I looked at my perfectly healed finger and smiled. My thoughts turned to my next destination. There was a hotel on the next block with a bar and escort girls so I went in that direction. When I got within half a block, the hawker in the doorway saw me and waved for me to come to him. My senses heightened. These guys were not to be trusted. To them, Americans were suckers with money.

"You come. I have number one girl for you. She love you long time," he said reaching for my sleeve.

I side-stepped him and in one long stride, I was inside. I scanned the place quickly. It was a typical American-looking bar with one difference. Ladies for hire sat along the wall on the side of the place most visible from the street. They sat expectantly, their faces tilted up as if in some school of etiquette and poise. Not wanting to appear too eager, I walked to the bar where I saw another American soldier seated talking to a woman sitting next to him. She sat leaning into him, seemingly very interested in everything he had to say. She was one of the bar girls. Her scarlet lipstick and pancake makeup gave her away. My intuition told me she was going through his money quickly. Having been brought up in New York City, I'd be harder to hustle. My friends and I had been approached by women of the night many times during our many adventures in Manhattan. This guy looked like a naïve corn-fed Midwesterner and I instinctively felt sorry for him. The bartender approached as I seated myself. I ordered a beer and when he returned with it, he started his sales pitch.

"You buy girl drink?" His eyes went to the women seated along the wall.

My opium girl Kwi.

"No" I answered. "Maybe, I buy girl for all night. You can do?"

"Yes, I can do," he answered

With that, the bargaining process began. I wound up choosing a girl based on congeniality rather than looks because they were all good-looking. I paid, bought a bottle of booze and we went upstairs.

That night was not filled with acrobatic sex or great debauchery. I knew it wouldn't be. The opium I had smoked inhibited all sexual pleasure and performance. We got to know each other and she told me about her children in one of the outlying villages. This was what she did to support them. We drank half the night and sat there laughing, naked and drunk, telling each other stories. We embraced. She told me I was beautiful. Then we slept. Very early in the morning, the sound of her getting dressed woke me. She had to go to her children. We embraced again, said our goodbyes, and I never saw her again.

26

Fall from Grace
and Ascent II

The barely rising sun defined the window coverings with a low gray glow. My pounding head fell to the pillow and I slept again. Some time passed and the clamor of Saigon woke me. It was time to get moving. Soon I'd be boarding a plane to Kuala Lumpur, but I wasn't very excited about it. I'd gone on R&R to Taiwan in 1968 and had been disappointed. The city struck me as rigid and conservative. The escorts that stayed with me presented formal and austere. Saigon had so much more to offer. Great times and genuinely affectionate girls could be found here. Unfortunately, the war made staying at Saigon overnight a punishable offense, and the MPs were always on the prowl for transgressors like me. Perhaps Kuala Lumpur would be more relaxed.

There was no telling who was out in the hall or downstairs so I dressed quietly and snuck downstairs. Vietnamese cops or American military police could be around and I didn't want to run into any of them. Vietnamese cops worked with MPs sometimes. The hotel staff smiled at me as I came downstairs. "You go now. No MP outside."

Grinning sheepishly, I walked across the lobby and slowly pushed the main door open. It seemed safe to go outside. Squinting in all directions I slid into the street. The heat of the city hit me full force as I left and it wasn't even noon yet. I ambled in the direction of the airbase. On the way, I met a street urchin selling drugs and I bought a few vials of heroin from him. Ducking into a doorway, I snorted one and dropped the other two into the side pocket of my jungle shirt. A cloud of anxiety hung over me as I headed towards the main gate of Tan Son Nhut. I imagined some authoritative sergeant at the R&R Center asking me where I'd been for two days. A minute later the trepidation was gone. The loving glow of heroin spread throughout my body and I basked in its wonderful cocoon. I looked down at the travel orders in my hand and I didn't give a damn if anyone wondered why I took so long. My Ranger beret made concocted convoluted stories believable. I hailed a cyclo and had the driver pedal towards the main gate.

I'd done this many times before back in 1968 while assigned to the 36th Engineer Battalion. There was nothing to it. One simply walked up to the gate, showed the AP (Air Police) travel orders, and walked through. Sometimes they waved you through without checking at all. This time, as I approached the gate, the gate guard's eyes locked on to me and stayed locked till I exited the vehicle. A panic-like instinct kicked in but I ignored it.

I should have never gotten off of that cyclo. I should've told the driver to keep pedaling but instead, I paid him, got off, and walked straight towards the guard and into the trap of my own making.

"Orders please." He never broke eye contact.

"Yup, right here."

He scanned the papers quickly. Then his eyes locked back onto mine and he said, "Please put your hands against this wall while I search you."

Everything drained from me. Even as I stabbed my hand into my pocket and threw the dope, I knew all was lost. The effort was futile and the dope landed in the dirt twenty feet away from me. Other Air Force cops appeared and retrieved it easily while the guard held me in place. I could have outrun them all easily but there is nowhere to go. I was done. In my mind, I was already picturing a court-martial, jail, and a dishonorable discharge. I felt faint. I didn't have to be told what to do. I knew to stay in the front leaning position, palms against the wall. It supported me on my wobbly legs. As my thoughts whirled, the wall felt like the last real thing in the world. Then the sergeant grabbed my wrists and locked them behind me in handcuffs. Shortly afterward, the wagon came and took me to the Air Force jail.

The Air Force jail and the holding cell I sat in gleamed surprisingly modern and comfortable. Freshly painted gray and white walls surrounded me inside my cell. Beyond the bars of my cell to the right stood an imposing desk. It towered at eye level just like the desk sergeant desks I'd seen as a kid when I'd gotten into trouble.

After some time, I relaxed enough to begin contemplating my situation. If I didn't find a way out of this, my life could be ruined. It was 1971 and though the handwriting was on the wall, the full scope of the public's indifference to the war, soldiers, and their discharges was yet to be understood, especially by those of us still in the military. I would go on to be a decorated war veteran with an honorable discharge, just to find that it counted for little in employment. In many cases, it was looked down on. That thin piece of paper was good only for VA benefits and federal employment. I'd later use it to go to school, but for now, bleak images of a dishonorable discharge, shame, and unemployment lurked behind all my waking thoughts.

Time passed. I stood, clutched the bars, and pressed my face between them. "Sergeant, I have to use the latrine."

"Someone will be right there." Skeptical eyes looked down on me from the desk.

Very shortly an AP came and escorted me to the latrine. I opened the door and almost froze. There, on top of the white commode, sat a black pistol belt replete with ammunition and revolver. My escort had already turned to leave so I made the split-second decision to enter. I had to quickly gauge this situation. I didn't want to get shot. An inexplicable mischievousness came over me and when I finished my business, I simply picked up the gun and pistol belt and walked out. The police desk was thirty feet or so away so I took giant strides to get to it quickly, all the time hugging the pistol belt so no one would see it. When I got there, I quickly laid it up on the desk and even more quickly withdrew my hand "Someone forgot this," I said. The desk sergeant said nothing. He stared at me like a statue: unable and unwilling to speak. I walked back to my cell and let myself in. Behind me, I'd left a bomb with a lit fuse. I, a prisoner had gotten his hands on a loaded gun due to negligence. I waited for the explosion but it never came. The matter was handled discreetly.

Shortly, a bus came for me and I was transferred to an army holding facility somewhere in Saigon. Two CIA types interviewed me to find out where I'd gotten the dope. They asked if I was dealing it: did I know any Vietcong, etc. The answer to everything was no, of course, and I found the question about knowing Vietcong particularly offensive. Eventually, I was locked in a cell and told someone from my unit would come to get me.

The cell had a steel bench for sleeping and nothing else. The dope in me slowly released its comforting hold and agitation and depression took its place. I focused on how exposed I'd be to any kind of attack. Through the bars, I could see Saigon beyond the compound I was locked in. Shrapnel from that direction could find its way to me easily because

I had no cover. I sat that way for three days: waiting in silence, my imagination running wild. Jangled nerves made sleep almost impossible and the steel bench proved many times more uncomfortable than the comparatively soft jungle floor I'd slept on so many times before. After three days, a sergeant from my new aviation unit came to get me. He reeked of booze and was clearly hungover. When I asked him where he'd been all this time, he replied with vague ambiguities that told me exactly where he'd been: he'd gone to party in Saigon for a few days just like I had. Anger welled up in me but I understood completely.

After some paperwork, I walked out of there with him a free man, but now it was time to face the music and before I knew it, I was on a plane back to Chu Lai.

When I arrived at my unit again, I was greeted with dismay and confusion. How could their brand-new Ranger acquisition be nothing more than a no-good doper? My cheeks burned with shame. I wished the Ranger patch on my shoulder was not there. I wished the meeting would end.

Not much was said. They assigned me sleeping quarters and I went directly to them. So began my lost days at Chu Lai. Nothing was asked of me and I gave nothing. My limbo-like status allowed me to roam wherever I wanted. The seashore at Chu Lai was a great escape and I spent many hours there staring into the water.

One day, as I sat there contemplating the beauty of the South China Sea and my bad situation, a figure appeared in the water on a raft. He had been hidden from view by the rocks or the derelict hulk of an old ship that had run aground there, but now he had floated out into my full view. I craned my neck to see him better and studied him carefully. At first, I thought he could be some sort of enemy scout. After all, this beach was deserted and all a person had to do to spy or perform acts of sabotage was exactly what he was doing. He could come ashore unnoticed. Slipping off the base would probably be even easier. My attention turned to his raft. To my great surprise, it was no more than five feet wide and perfectly round. Concave in shape, it allowed for about nine inches of draft and the water-line lay a perilous few inches below the sides. The man had one oar. He was dressed in a white shirt and black pants. I continued staring at him fascinated when I realized he was fishing with a hand line. Somehow, this man maneuvered his boat around the rocks with the paddle while simultaneously holding a hand line he worked with the other hand. Several minutes passed and he hooked a fish. His movements became acrobatic and balanced as he struggled to control the raft and the fish. From time to time he'd balanced down to the floor of the raft creating a tripod with one hand and both feet while he played the fish with the other hand. This went on for several minutes and at one point he disappeared from view. Finally, he pulled it up. The fish was almost three feet long. It gleamed in the sun like a mirror when it moved. The man tended to it. It appeared he was tying a rope to it.

Suddenly I saw movement to my left. Two MPs appeared and were moving quickly towards the water. They had left their Jeep on the road up above the rocks and I knew immediately they were going for this fisherman. As soon as they reached the rocks they motioned with their arms for the fisherman to come in. They made their way down towards the water and continued waving their arms at him. Slowly and reluctantly the fisherman made his way to shore next to them. His face appeared worn and sullen. He most probably had taken his chances and lost by fishing there. He had to go with them for questioning. I wondered what would become of the fish and soon had my answer. He would not leave it. He argued loudly with the MPs though I could not hear him well enough to understand what he was saying or in what language. In the end, to my shock and delight, they let him bring the fish and the three of them walked off with it towards the Jeep.

Sea birds, boulders, and that rusting, abandoned freighter there in the water always captivated me and gave me some escape. I'd sit staring at that rotting vessel thinking about what a majestic ocean-going machine it must have been at one time. Misdirection, propulsion failure, or perhaps a tropical storm had caused it to founder and wash up on the rocky beach here. Now it would sit pounded by the sea and ground by salt, sand, and wind till someday nothing but pieces remained ... a desolate destiny. The wreck reminded me of my situation in the aviation company. I had to become an expert at being invisible. Time passed comfortably this way but I found it moved more slowly. What would my legacy be? If I made it to an honorable discharge I'd have to look at myself for the rest of my life. The wreck that got stuck and sat uncomfortably on the rocks. After all, I had come here to become a door gunner on a helicopter. I thought about it some more but it was time to go buy some more dope because malcontentedness and anxiety crept slowly towards me again.

Sometimes I'd shop at the PX, small as it was, or wander the base. It was a good way to meet mammasans. They brought in plenty of dope and I used more and more of it as time passed. As the weeks slipped into months, I realized that I was far from the only one using dope. The sands around our company area at Chu Lai shifted with winds and hurried boots. They rearranged constantly. Empty heroin vials hidden and discarded there revealed themselves daily. It seemed half the company—an aviation company—was using dope. Though I couldn't escape my guilty feelings, I felt better knowing there were many like me getting high … but I knew something was very wrong here … with the war … with me… The gnawing dread I'd always felt showed itself again when I thought about these things.

Boredom grew as an annoying, malcontent weight on my consciousness, and still, nobody asked me to report to any job. The war had lost all relevance to me and time slowed even more.

The days blur here at Chu Lai and I'm still grappling with the fact that just a month ago I was a proud Ranger. Now I'm known, in an aviation company, as the lowlife who got caught with heroin. I am worried because at some point there will be a court-martial. Nobody has said anything to me yet but I know the Army is not going to let this slide. I try not to be conspicuous. I indulge myself in the misguided fantasy that if I am not seen, nothing will happen. Today I'm going to kill some time by going to the small PX that sits half a mile from our hooches. It's a small PX with only bare necessities like toothbrushes and shaving cream.

The building is elevated so I take two steps up to enter it. Inside, five or six men mill about the dimly lit interior. None of them seem to be shopping in earnest. Their mindset, as they meander around the poorly stocked shelves, seems to be the same as mine: getting away, if just for a little while. The clerk at the register looks bored.

The sudden sound is familiar to me. It almost sounds like an owl but not really. It is a 122mm rocket two to three seconds before impact. I hear the sound as it begins before it intensifies. I almost have enough time to warn everyone inside. I can see only a couple are aware of what is about to happen. By then the sound is at its loudest and a fraction of a second later the rocket impacts. At that moment all eyeballs turn to me for some reason. Perhaps it is because I am still framed inside the doorway.

"Everyone get out and get down!" I yell as loudly as I can. Then I bound out and down the steps, throwing myself into the lowest spot of dirt I can find by the road. As the other men are hitting the dirt around me, I lift my head and swivel around. I can see the plume of smoke rising from where the rocket hit some distance from me. I can't be sure but it looks like the rocket hit the dispensary. It is a building usually bustling with medics and people needing minor medical attention for cuts, fevers, infections, and the like. At first, I considered going there but then I think better of it. If they have a spotter, the enemy will know that his first shot was spot on and he may repeat it.

I stay in the area and observe from a distance as the dead and wounded are carried out. Though I feel a sense of great sadness and empathy for the men who were in that building, the feeling is overridden by the gratitude I feel for that rocket not having landed by me.

Later that afternoon I walked back to the dispensary. I can tell from the gigantic hole in the roof that the rocket exploded there and not on the floor. Walking closer I can see two-by-four building lumber snapped in two. There are scraps of human tissue adhering to the blasted rubble. I can stand to look no more and I turn to leave.

Days passed and the news came suddenly. We were ordered to pack up and be ready to move the next day. We were given no details and ordered not to speak of what little we thought we knew. In the morning we'd be getting on trucks and helicopters. The destination was Quang Tri, a city almost within walking distance of North Vietnam. The news sobered me. Sleep was difficult that night and in the morning, two companies loaded up on vehicles and helicopters and moved out. Non-aviators went on trucks and the rest went with their respective birds. I hopped on a truck with little more than my rifle and soon we began moving.

The line of trucks ahead of mine bobbed, bounced, and swayed from side to side: a cartoonish vision leading me towards my possible demise. Black smoke belched from diesel engines and sand dust blew from beneath the vehicles. We were barely twenty miles out of the city of Chu Lai and already the wooden bench of the deuce-and-a-half (2½ ton truck) I sat on started getting uncomfortable. The hard wooden slats repeatedly struck my butt. I tried to settle in to find a comfortable position but nothing worked. My helmet cranked my head with each bounce so I took it off and stashed it under the seat on someone's duffel bag. It was going to be a long ride.

Our convoy snaked through valleys, hamlets, and over bridges. We moved northwest through occasional checkpoints in the road manned by graven, somber ARVN soldiers. Their tired gray faces sobered us. Slowly but surely the sun set behind a large hill we'd been driving towards. The old familiar knot in my chest welled up again just below my throat. We were about to drive over a mountain in the dark. A bunch of cooks, clerks, mechanics, and other assorted noncombatants were about to drive over a mountain, in the dark, in a bad part of Vietnam.

We entered the woods past the last hamlet, after the last checkpoint. Trees closed in on us tightly on both sides of the road. This was a perfect site for an ambush but the area had probably been cleared by American or Vietnamese forces. I hoped for that as we rumbled through that forest. After a while, the trees began to thin and the road began to sound more gravelly. We were starting up the mountain on a crude road blasted and carved into the side of it. Diesel engines screamed louder, gears ground under stubborn fists on gear shifters and rocks popped under the great tires. Beneath our convoy, the earth dropped farther and farther away. We were about to cross the notorious Hai Van Pass.

The higher we rode, the rougher the road felt. I looked around and craned my head down to see truck tires way too close to an edge that could be our most certain demise, yet higher we traveled higher still. I'd look over again but then turn my head back to the inside of the truck. Seeing the expressions on the other faces gave a comfort, a false sense of security that was better than looking into the ever-deepening chasm below us. We rode this way in the dark with a shared, understood tension. I'd seen this before: helplessness and resolve on faces steadfastly approaching danger. My thoughts kept turning to the driver. My life depended on him and I didn't like the idea.

Eventually, the truck leveled out and I looked around to realize we were at the top of the mountain. Village lights glowed as pinpoints in the distant black horizon. Relief flooded over us. I could see it in the others' faces. We rolled on steadily and after a while, we noticed a perceptible dip of the front of our truck. The roar of the engines changed to an uncompliant whine of gears. We were descending. The bouncing resumed. We drove down the mountain with the truck's nose down and that was even more unnerving than the ride up. The chasm on my side of the truck glowed black again like a heinous maw. Every new bounce of the truck struck a new chord of fear. My hands gripped the railing and the bench as we rolled down even faster … faster … why were we going faster? The jostling and bumps of the ride increased in frequency to the point we felt them less. Our speed increased even more and I realized something was wrong. Wheels bounced closer to the edge of the road. The speed of the bouncing caused sway in the back of the truck. I could feel we were jumping left to right a few inches at a time. Faster we went. I stood up to see what was going on, barely keeping my balance. It seemed like we were going forty miles an hour ... way too fast for a mountain road.

I realized the truck was out of control. Other guys realized it too. They began standing, wide-eyed looking in all directions and falling back to their seat. Still, we accelerated. I considered jumping out of the truck when the banging started. The driver had turned his wheels into the mountain and we ran down it in a succession of crashes that eventually slowed us and then stopped us. Though stunned, we quickly unloaded and moved forward to get on other trucks.

I looked back one last time at the black, villainous, dead behemoth I had almost ridden to my death. We drove without incident to the bottom of the mountain and eventually stopped to regroup near a small village.

My back is against a truck tire. Some guys are standing around but I don't want to make that large a target of myself. We all look at each other when we hear the voices. They were not American and I quickly crane my head to see what was going on. The residents of the hamlet were streaming out of the darkness to see us. Sometimes this could be a cause for concern but my gut told me it wasn't this time. These people were happy to see us. They stood smiling and laughing as we engaged them in conversation. A particularly attractive female came up to me, leaned in, and asked me if I wanted sex. My eyes widened and I smiled at her. At twenty-four, I never refused sex. The deal was quickly sealed and I chose one of the cabs of the trucks to engage in our liaison. All thought and caution were lost in my youthful lust. Before the deed could be finished I heard raucous laughter outside the truck. Then it stopped suddenly. I looked up and out the window to see a lieutenant glaring into the cab.

"Get out of there." He ordered us out of the truck and shooed the woman away. When he left, I scowled at the guys.

"What's the matter with you guys? Why couldn't you be cool? Your laughing like idiots is what alerted the lieutenant," I said.

"Sorry man, your white ass going up and down in the cab of the truck was too funny." I had to laugh through my frustration.

We Had to Get Out of That Place

Several minutes later we saddled up the trucks again and though we'd only completed half of our journey, the rest of it seemed insignificant after the loss of our brakes on Hai Van pass. We drove on and finally entered the U.S. military compound at Quang Tri.

Besides being dreary and cold, Quang Tri sat dangerously close to North Vietnam and the NVA. It was so cold that we were issued down feather sleeping bags. We slept on concrete in an incomplete hospital construction project: a children's hospital no less. It looked as though the project had stopped in midstream. I'd look around those walls and wonder how altruistic ideals could take their shape as floors and walls in a setting of such madness. Perhaps this children's hospital was one of the many military projects meant to win hearts and minds. The walls afforded us some protection from shrapnel in the case of rocket or mortar attacks. The place quickly became unhappy and depressing for us. There were no smiling mammasans milling about the company area and we had few of the creature comforts of the barracks in Chu Lai. Once again I practiced my art of staying out of everyone's way. Heroin proved more difficult to find here than at Chu Lai. Fewer civilians worked here and the ones that I could find were more resistant to being approached. Still, I persisted, and after I scored I'd hang in the shadows and peripheries of my unit.

It was out back of my company area at another section of the unfinished hospital that I met Kiet. Kiet was a patient at the hospital even though it was not finished yet. He was a little kid that stood barely past my knee. He was always naked and spoke no English. He wore a cast embedded with a rod from the waist to his left arm. The purpose of the rod was to hold his arm up. I was told Kiet had bone cancer. I'd visit him every day and bring him apples. In this grim and severe place, Kiet brought me joy and light. Meanwhile, the rest of my guys were working. Most were flying. The malaise fell over me again. I felt useless and I knew that if I continued this, I would be found out by everyone and exposed as being a bum. I did not much like myself anyway so one day I did a good snort of heroin, walked up to the commanding officer, and said, "Sir, I came here to be a door gunner. I'd like a chance to do that."

The whole thing went surprisingly easy. He didn't ask me much. Mostly, he just looked me over, granted my request, and excused me. A day and a half later I was summoned to take a flight physical. The only part that I had any difficulty with had to do with eye reaction time and I

Kiet: the orphan with bone cancer.

failed that by one point because I was high on heroin. I was put on flight status anyway.

    We flew every day. I don't remember any days off. The endless flying made the time pass quickly and I used less dope but I got shot at my first day flying, and in one month of doing this job, I would have closer brushes with death than any other time in my two tours of Vietnam.

27

"Mayday, Mayday"

If you are in trouble anywhere in the world, an airplane can fly over and drop flowers, but a helicopter
can land and save your life.—Igor Sikorsky, Helicopter pioneer

The sound of their approach generated excitement. Their power as
they descended elicited awe. They took us into battle and in the din of
destruction, we could call on them for help. Often, through our tears,
we'd watch one fly away with a friend we'd never see again. They flew in
with whirling wings as avenging angels on the battlefield. They rained
fire and death on the enemy and after the fight, they'd bring us home.
Later, as we sat in stunned reflection, they'd bring us beer and our mail.
We admired and respected them. Some of us yearned to soar up there
with them. I was enthralled by these heroes in the sky. I wanted to be
one of them. I asked for door-gunner duty and got it.

Though many soldiers volunteered for door-gunner duty in Vietnam. Most gunners got the job by assignment after formal training in
Fort Rucker, Alabama. I was chosen because of my combat experience
and, though I didn't know it yet, every available hand was needed for the
upcoming invasion of Laos. My adulation of these aviators blinded me
to the obvious. This was dangerous duty. Half of the helicopters in Vietnam got destroyed in combat.

I took a flight physical and the next day I was issued a fire-retardant
flight suit, leather boots, a flight helmet, and a machine gun. The day
after that, I reported to my assigned helicopter.

With the weight of my M60 machine gun pushing down on my
left shoulder, I walked towards the runway trying to appear casual.
Self-consciousness and anxiety shortened my steps and probably gave
me away. The anxious feeling dulled a brilliant morning. Once again, I

dreaded the prospect of not performing properly when the time came; just as I had in the infantry and Rangers. Though relatively simple, the steps gunners and crew chiefs had to follow on takeoffs and landings were critically important. Other details preoccupied me as well. Among my responsibilities was tying down the helicopter's blades on shutdown and fueling the helicopter while adhering to a strict protocol (which was rarely followed). All in all, the sum of these rattled me. I had to get this right because, for a while, all eyes would be on me. As if performance anxiety wasn't enough, the idea of flying across the border and landing by the Ho Chi Minh trail bothered me. Till now, the Laos operation had been kept secret.

It seemed to me that my entire time in the Army I'd had to bob and weave to have some control over my fate. I felt that if I left my fate in the hands of the Army, I'd wind up with crappy assignments or in a body bag. Now here I was flying right into the jaws of the enemy; in Laos no less. I don't know if my maneuvering worked or if I kept jumping out of the frying pan into the fire. The most dangerous situations of two tours in Vietnam were to follow, but I'd live to write about them. I don't know if I'd be here today, had I not taken the actions I had, despite the danger they landed me in. I juggled fate but I lived to tell the tale.

I approached the helicopter. Despite its dull olive color, it gleamed its lines and hues at me, almost as if beckoning me. The flat, diamond-patterned, silvery floor shone brightly and airiness about the bird became even more apparent as I looked through one door and out the other. I'd been in many helicopters before, but this was the first time I paid attention to all the details.

The bench seat I'd be gunning from sat recessed in the bird, slightly to the rear of the middle of the right side. In front of my seat, an aluminum rod curved up and out from the bird. I'd be mounting my M60 machine gun on it. The thought that I'd be partially responsible for up to ten lives and an aircraft that cost upwards of a quarter of a million dollars humbled me.

Our crew chief (port side door gunner), Baggett, gave me a short orientation and we took off in a formation of ten birds. We never really spoke again.

"Clear up right," I said, as I leaned out watching my side of the helicopter.

"Clear up left," Baggett announced in turn.

I listened to every word I heard over the intercom carefully and studied every feature we flew over as if cramming for a test. I paid close attention to everything as it unfolded and tried to memorize every detail of my job as I learned it: loading, refueling, landings, takeoffs.

"Crossing the fence."

The pilot's words sobered me. We had just flown over the Vietnam-Laos border. That imaginary line made everything feel different. It was in fact different. Here divisions of NVA troops operated with impunity. I tried to peer into every feature in the landscape beneath me. We flew over a large expanse of tree-dotted, plain-like terrain. I wanted to see into those trees, but we were too high for that.

I wondered about .51 caliber machine guns and Russian or Chinese anti-aircraft weapons. We flew in silence listening to chatter on the intercom when transmission from another bird came through our commo channels. "Mayday, Mayday, Going down on fire."

The words stunned me. I'd heard them before in war movies. A bird ahead of us had gotten hit and was descending out of control and aflame. The worst-case scenario had just manifested itself in six words; the direst words I'd heard in almost two years of combat duty. I looked at the pilot. He briefly glanced at the co-pilot. Somewhere ahead of us a man might be falling to his death. Nothing was said and we droned on. Less than a minute passed and "Beeper, Beeper, come up voice," came through my headphones. The words repeated intermittently. I instinctively knew what they meant though they were explained to me later. Somewhere on the ground, someone was trying to establish contact with a bird that had gone down.

When a helicopter crashed in Vietnam, the pilot used a radio transmitter that beeped a signal. It also had voice capabilities. "Come up voice" meant "talk to me."

He never came up voice. I have often wondered if those guys made it.

28

Down Behind the Lines

Darkness bloomed into glowing dawn on the Quang Tri runway. We took off like gods riding whirling, winged, green dragons. Suited green and bug-eyed looking with our helmet visors down, we felt secure in the throbbing beasts we were buckled and strapped into. Electronic umbilical communication cords ran from the back of our flight helmets directly into the bird's main system. I could talk to anybody in our flight crew with a push of a button. With a turn of the channel selector switch, I could speak to people on the ground.

The giant formation of helicopters lifted into the airy chasm that was the passageway to Laos. I felt invincible. As a former ground soldier, being armed with my own personal helicopter and attached machine gun imbued me with a false sense of omnipotence. My fireproof Nomex flight suit fit me neatly. I admired the skin-tight fit of the leather-palmed, Nomex gloves I gripped my M60 machine gun with. My communication helmet was more unique and sharp-looking than any piece of equipment the Army had ever issued me. Its tinted visor hid most of my face. I could see everyone but they couldn't see me. I was bad to the bone and felt better in this attire than any suit I'd ever owned. I fit the helicopter and it fit me. It had a flying machine gun platform with two expert getaway drivers.

"Coming up." The pilot's announcement produced instant adrenalin..

"Clear up right," I replied, with some authority, after checking my side of the bird.

"Clear up left," said the other gunner (crew chief).

JP4 (aviation fuel) fumes perfumed the thunder of our assault force and radio transmissions regarding our flight chattered through our helmets.

"Wind west at seven knots. Clouds at 9,000 feet. Depart runway at your discretion."

We Had to Get Out of That Place

With that, we took off. Overwhelming sensations of wind, whirling blades, and arching helicopters augmented my pumping blood with even more adrenalin. I felt energized and more alive than I had in a long time. The formation of Huey UH1 helicopters slowly lifted into the sky along with an escort of gunship attack helicopters. They vibrated under their respective crews roaring a challenge to the rising sun and the day behind it. We were invincible. We were coming and you didn't want to be in our way.

Our flight was a rescue mission. Operation Lam Son 719, the invasion of Laos, was in full swing. We'd been delivering ARVN (Army of the Republic of Vietnam) soldiers and special operations forces for days. Previous flights had some of their birds, including Witchdoctor 5, shot down. Alone in Laos, the crew sat amid enemy troops and hid in an abandoned bunker according to what I'd heard. After days of incessant airstrikes and extraction attempts, they were rescued by ARVN Rangers. This flight, one of my first, was a rescue mission.

In the coming weeks, I'd be the one getting rescued...

Pilots pulled pitch and the familiar nose down, forward lift pushed me into my seat. We picked up speed. I realized I had to temper my excitement and awe to keep my perspective and senses alert for the job ahead. The staccato roar on the runway rose in intensity to a low scream as we flew off the airfield at Quang Tri. Through the din, clear words flowed sharply through the wires in my helmet.

"Gunner, you been briefed about our mission?" The pilot asked.

"Our crew chief told me a little, sir."

"Well, when we hit the deck in Laos, be real careful with that '60 [M60 Machine Gun]. This thing could play out a dozen different ways. Don't go hot [command to fire] unless I tell you to."

"Yes, sir."

Sunlight and cool air bathed me. The loose end of my seatbelt danced crazily, slapping every surface it could find. I made a mental note to tuck it away in the future, a mistake that would almost cost me my life. Quang Tri slid away and we climbed to get out of the 50 to 1,000 foot danger zone that was considered "dead man's altitude."

We leveled off at a few thousand feet. If we ever changed course for a heading correction off the runways, I never noticed. We were charging hard westward towards Laos and I don't believe we ever stopped to refuel. Usually, flights into the Laos combat zones and the Ho Chi Minh Trail refueled at Khe Sanh or Lang Vei. We were flying straight in.

28. Down Behind the Lines

I felt so clean, so much a part of the bird I was flying in. Sunlight glinted off metal surfaces that were spotless before a flight and blown cleaner during it. Every part of the ship was latched, hatched, or secured with snaps and straps of every sort. The pilots' consoles dazzled me with their complexity and the sheer number of instruments neatly crammed against each other. It beamed as an artistic mosaic: an astounding visual of complicated technology. There had to be at least a hundred dials, gauges, buttons, and levers within both pilots' reach, over their heads, under them, forward of them, and behind them. Even the cables leading into our helmets had control buttons.

We droned on towards Laos. The jungle stretched as far as I could see. I leaned out over my seat and looked straight down at least a mile. I relied on my seat belt to hold me in because without it I could have fallen into the jungle below. In my youth, I'd almost died by slipping off a rocky precipice. I usually had a fear of heights but it was gone now. I felt one with the helicopter.

I swung my helmeted head from left to right, craning it to see if I could make out anything in the dark spaces between the trees in the green jungle below me, feeling keenly aware that the lush forests below me hid regiments of North Vietnamese troops. The ever-present question was, "Where?"

I kept my machine gun pointed away from the demonic looking gunships that buzzed around our formation. Their presence lent some assurance with their bristling weaponry. Their painted-on teeth proclaimed their power. I had great respect for the crews in those birds. They could level a village in minutes or save us in an emergency situation. Their missions were almost always hot. We'd be relying on these birds of prey when we were on the ground in Laos. I waved at one of them as it flew by but I'm sure the pilots never noticed. They were too busy constantly scanning for targets, though any targets were well concealed by the thick jungle. Endless waves of jungle awed me as valleys dipped from hills and I was struck by the lack of any type of city or village in the wilderness below me. We were approaching the western side of the north part of Vietnam. Any signs of civilization had been erased by the ravages of war long ago. But for the scars that left, this place was as God had created it.

This was also the area of the notorious Khe Sanh siege of '68. Now firefights raged daily around Khe Sanh and its outposts. It was critical as a staging area for the invasion of Laos.

"Look sharp guys, we're getting close," came over my headphones.
"Roger," I replied.

A growing knot had formed in my stomach. The pilot announced that we had "crossed the fence" into Laos. I got on my M60 with tighter fingers than usual. My butt raised off the bench and I leaned out the door a little further. The endless forests had given way to a mottled jungle with many clearings with threatening wood-lines. Anyone could take a shot at us from this scattered landscape and duck back into its hiding places for cover. For now, however, we flew high enough to be relatively safe. We were in Laos and it felt like it. I could feel real or imagined tension from the other ships. If one was to go down in Laos, there would be no cavalry to rescue them. They'd have to rely on their own aviation unit to get them out. It felt as though we were off the charts on another planet. We really were totally on our own now.

I snapped out of my absorbed state as I realized we were losing altitude. Trees and features of the Laotian landscape were getting bigger. Laos was coming up at me as a threatening grand finale to our flight. I felt we were picking up airspeed as we descended because the rotors and engines seemed to roar louder. We were moving faster. Suddenly, we descended further in a gigantic swoop. Our escort birds came to life in a symphony of machine gun fire, rockets, and grenades. Both flanks of our formation were blasted. Explosions, flashes of light, and smoke peppered the landscape in my immediate field of vision. At first, I felt fright, then awe. Then I found myself speculating whether we might get hit by our own shrapnel. I knew we were violating all ordnance safety rules.

As I tensed madly on my gun, I waited for an order to fire that never came. At this point, the ground was thirty feet below us. I saw nothing but jungle through my squinted, scanning eyes. We hovered there stock still over the ground of Laos for what seemed an eternity but it was only ten seconds or so. Then we simply took off again. It seemed to me we left as soon as we'd arrived. I didn't know what transpired on the ground, I only heard assorted stories later.

The flight back to Vietnam was uneventful but no one spoke. We were not home yet. When the pilot announced we were crossing the fence again, I felt a great relief wash over me though we still were in a notoriously bad part of Vietnam. We worked our way back to Quang Tri. There I was told the story of our somewhat anticlimactic adventure. I don't know how much the story changed by the time it was told to me. Accounts varied. I never saw the crewman one of our birds picked up. I did not see anything because I'd been too busy on my M60. I never saw a pick-up bird on the ground either. All I remember is peering intently at the dark spaces between trees and behind bushes. I was told back at Quang Tri that the crewman that had been picked up had been hiding in a vacant North Vietnamese bunker, with enemy troops nearby. He could not come out for fear of getting killed by them. We came down in force and plucked him out of his situation. I tell this story the way I remember it. I did little research for these stories. This is the way I remember it. This is the way I'm telling it. Many accounts differ.

29

Lines in the Sky

We must be flying two miles up. It feels great up here. We are so far up, the jungle looks like the top of a stalk of broccoli. I let go of my M60 and let it droop down on its stand. We are flying out of dead man's altitude now. At this height, we can't be hit by most rifle fire. I turn around to look at the six guys sitting on the cargo floor. These are not regular ARVNs. They have confidence and smugness about them. The smuggest one, and obvious leader of these men, conveys subtle amusement: like the quarterback in school sitting among the girls who think he's hot ... but this has nothing to do with his looks. He is bad to the bone and he knows it. I know it too. I understand it better the moment I see the snarling black cat patch on his shoulder. He is a Vietnamese Ranger, U.S. trained. Either they have a shortage of uniforms or they had more pride than common sense. Getting captured with that patch meant torture and certain death. On all my own Ranger missions we wore no ID or patch for that very reason.

We'd gotten briefed on the mission back at Khe Sanh after refueling. A hill in Laos had been bombarded by artillery all night in preparation and we were told we were going to drop a team of South Vietnamese soldiers on it. I hadn't gotten the scoop that they were Rangers. Now I finally had got chance to get a good look at them. I studied them. These guys were specialists: professionals on a professional mission. That meant there was a heightened probability of making contact with the enemy. My stomach knotted into the familiar ready mode. Hot LZs were the situation most deadly to helicopter crews. There was nothing I could do but steel myself.

A lonely silence marked our straight line into Laos. For me, flying unescorted always felt a little like being lost. I turned to the team in my bird to see if they were making any preparations. They were not, they were completely ready to go. They simply sat, stone-faced with blackened faces, taped gear, and unbelievably, their Ranger patches.

We're descending. I lift the cover of my '60 and remove the ammo belt. I work the bolt a few times before I re-insert it. Then, I snap the cover firmly into place again.

My right hand slides down my stomach to the seat belt and gives it a good yank. It is loose. I lean taut against it, daring it not to hold me as I angle my body in the Laotian sky to get a good view below and ahead. I see a hill ahead but not much else. We're going in at a steep angle. I dart my eyes in all directions including down. When I look back up the mountain again I see something behind it. I can't make it out. It looks like a white elongated shape in the sky. Now it's getting longer ... longer still. It's clear to me that a straight white vertical line is developing in the sky and it's getting longer, heading towards the ground. I peer intently at it, wondering what I'm looking at, not sure of what I am seeing. As I stare incredulous, I see another line is beginning to form to the left of it. About the time the first line is almost to the ground and the second line is about halfway, a third line begins to form. This continues in a sort of symmetry as I watch transfixed. By now, most of the lines have made it to the ground and are getting thicker and thicker. By the time we're a couple of thousand feet over our hilltop destination, about ten lines have all connected into a solid wall of white. It is a smoke-screen, a curtain of solid white, the likes of which I have never seen or heard of before. I think it is the Air Force doing this to cover our descent onto the hill. I scan the sky carefully but I can see no plane.

"Gunners, stay cold (don't fire) unless you take fire." It was the pilot.

"Got it."

As the hill below comes up at us, I realize it is destroyed, devoid of any life. All the trees are black and twisted, a shattered tangled mess. I smell the acrid residue of high explosives. I think I see smoke among these splintered trees. Our passengers are in the doors getting ready to jump. We have to hover to find a decent spot to put them in. There is no way a man can jump into what I see before me without injuring himself.

We finally found a suitable clear spot between a few broken trees. They quickly jumped out of the bird and we lifted off. I found myself gazing at them forlornly, the way guys look at their family at railroad stations when the train he put them on pulls out of the station. I watched them as we rose away from them till they were nothing more than scurrying specs on that hill. They never looked back at us. The probability is that they never made it out of there alive because Operation Lam Son 719 was a disaster for the South Vietnamese Army.

Poor, brave sons-of-bitches.

30

Redemption at Lang Vei

I'd been flying as a door gunner on UH-1H helicopters for almost a month. What started as a glory and adventure fantasy that would keep me out of the infantry, quickly degraded into bleak reality. Again, it seemed, I was jumping out of the frying pan into the fire. Flying into enemy territory daily was as dangerous as anything I'd done in Vietnam. I was not the only one feeling the strain of the flights in and out of Laos. Anxiety and fear had replaced the happy-go-lucky demeanor of our guys. Anyone could easily see the new lines on the faces of our aircrews at our temporary headquarters in Quang Tri. We flew every day, sometimes into the night. I don't remember any days off. Despite the danger, endless flying made the time pass quickly and I used less dope.

Just before takeoff, I clicked my seatbelt closed, took the long loose end, and wrapped it snugly around the rest of it so it would not flap wildly in the wind. These seatbelts were made "one-size-fits-all" and my twenty-eight-inch waist allowed for three feet of the excess belt to blow crazily in all directions when we flew. It was annoying and probably unsafe.

Warm winds whipped about me in the gunner's seat that day and sun sparkled in our aircraft. Panoramic vistas stretched out below us. The unique green that was Vietnam stretched out as far as the eye could see. We weren't flying missions into Laos that day. Maybe we'd finished early and had been flying mail runs or other non-combat missions. Either way, I remember a distinct lightness of mood in the aircraft. A steady stream of banter from the pilots flowed through my communications helmet. The unbroken expanse of lush, green treetops mottled the jungle below us. It always mesmerized me. If I considered the fact that it was where the enemy hid, I quickly dismissed the thought. Great weather and the lack of enemy engagement made for a great day of flying so far. We enjoyed the moment. Time moved quickly and easily.

30. Redemption at Lang Vei

The tone of the pilots' conversations changed. They suddenly sounded quizzical and absorbed. Our airspeed decreased. Both pilots' heads craned downward, looking at the ground. Though I didn't know it yet, we were flying a circle over a former refueling stop that had been abandoned. It sat near an old base named Lang Vei. The flattened square contrasted with the greenery of the jungle around it. It had been abandoned because the North Vietnamese Army (NVA) kept hitting it with sniper and mortar fire from the surrounding hills. Lang Vei sat almost squarely on the Ho Chi Minh trail just southwest of Khe Sanh where the North Vietnamese Army had massed against our Marines in 1968. The borders of North Vietnam, South Vietnam, and Laos met just miles from there. When we flew in a southerly direction, I could see in the distance the river that was the border between Vietnam and Laos. Lang Vei was the site of a former Special Forces base that had been attacked repeatedly and eventually overrun in 1968 by NVA troops with tanks. The Marines had considered helping them but couldn't because of the probability of being ambushed. Vietnam didn't get any worse than Lang Vei.

The pilots chatted and mused about landing to retrieve a fire extinguisher that had been left there in haste during the desertion of the base. I vaguely recall talk of trading it for a case of steaks. Apparently the mess sergeant (main cook) was short of fire extinguishers, which regulations required. I stiffened as a bolt of fear shot through me. Disdain and disbelief mingled with dread. Surely they were not serious. The very thought of landing there seemed ridiculous. To my relief, they straightened out the bird and we left. A deep breath escaped me and relief swept over me as I settled back and eyed Laos in the distance. Lang Vei slid away beneath us.

I relaxed. Warm wind and tropical sun soothed me as I leaned on my M60 machine gun. We flew at a safe altitude, high in the sky. So far the only danger that day had been takeoffs and landings. Of course, the possibility of getting shot down by 37mm anti-aircraft fire was always in the back of our minds, but this danger occurred mostly over Laos. These weapons used targeting radar. I was told if I heard clicks or beeping while over Laos, it was radar locking in on the bird and that I'd be dead by the third beep. The Army taught many last-ditch methods for dealing with deadly situations like ambushes or rocket attacks, but there was little in the books for dealing with getting blown up a mile up in the air. Fortune favored us. We never heard that radar sound.

We Had to Get Out of That Place

The day progressed without incident. Landings, take-offs, drop-offs, and pick-ups ... we flew around the Khe Sanh plateau among the many outposts manned by American and ARVN troops. Some were larger unit-sized encampments; some were smaller forward positions where we'd hover and never actually touch down. The area teemed with NVA troops and Viet Cong guerrillas. The smaller outposts and observation positions often got hit. It was easy to take a bullet or two while coming down onto one of these hilltops or fighting positions. During these landings and takeoffs, I'd be on my gun and sharp. I always felt bad for the soldiers manning these deadly posts. We'd often recover their dead after they got hit during the night.

Once we picked up an ambush team that had been very successful. They'd killed a mess of gooks and got on board grinning and carrying a load of captured weapons and explosives. I winced at the thought of what could happen flying around with this cheaply made Chinese weaponry. I always feared it could explode because it had been booby-trapped or armed. As a Ranger, I'd learned to be wary of retrieved enemy weaponry, especially high explosives. Many men in Vietnam died by picking up or even touching found or captured enemy armament. An RPG detonating in-flight could incinerate a helicopter in mid-air.

We picked up a black soldier somewhere along the way. I didn't know where he was going; probably back to a rear area or Khe Sanh. In Vietnam, most casual travel was done by helicopter. If a soldier needed to go someplace, he simply asked the crew members of any helicopter if they had room. I remember the guy jumping into the bird and little else. I wasn't paying much attention. I was listening to the rhythmic beat of rotor blades. We flew on.

It dawned on me slowly that we were over that deserted square in the jungle again. The pilots were talking about the fire extinguisher again. Everything snapped back into a sharp focus as I turned my head to look at them. I felt the same twinge of foreboding as before. From the tone of their voice, I could tell these guys seemed to feel it was no big deal to make an unauthorized landing in enemy territory without anybody knowing about it. We banked and changed direction to circle the clearing. I can't remember what was said. My eyes were glued on the ominous, rectangular area we were circling. I couldn't believe we were going down there.

We lost altitude and the former fuel stop come up at us. In no time at all, the ground loomed beneath us as the pilot adjusted his stick to touch down softly. The helicopter's skids bumped the ground and there we were. It suddenly felt like no big deal. We sat on a perfectly flat landing area. If I didn't know better, I'd think we were in some rear area. I no longer felt uncomfortable because my senses betrayed me. Piece of cake; land on the familiar-looking, man-made flat-top, grab the fire extinguisher, and go.

Baggett, the other gunner, and Crew Chief, jumped out of the bird on the other side. The fire extinguisher lay several feet away, though I couldn't see it because it was on the right side of the bird. I expected to only be there only a few seconds and lift off again.

What happened next, I can only describe as a loss of consciousness for a fraction of a second. I don't remember the explosion, only the ringing in my head immediately afterward. I never passed out, but I don't remember any concussion either. It took a second or two to react to the sound in my ears. I heard what I can only liken to a giant ringing—the sound one would hear if their head was in a church bell and someone hit it with a sledgehammer. I did not hear the strike, only the ringing afterward. The sound penetrated to the core of my being. It stunned and immobilized me with its suddenness and intensity. Those two seconds stretched out into a short eternity. I snapped back to reality about the same time everyone else did. I turned to look at the pilots. One of them hit the stick. The engine screamed as we did an immediate lift-off. The aircraft lurched forward and up. Within seconds we were twenty to forty feet in the air. Wide-eyed and dumbstruck, I struggled to make sense of what was happening when I saw the black passenger jump out of the helicopter. He just jumped right out. His exit was not unlike a skydiver's. He did not tip, slip or fall. He deliberately positioned himself squarely in the open door of our helicopter and jumped out. In disbelief and shock, I was watching the situation get worse by the second. I looked out the door and down and saw him below lying motionless on the ground. Now we had an injured or dead man to recover.

We were still gaining altitude when I realized that in addition to our jumper, we had another problem. We'd left Baggett on the ground. All I remember clearly is leaning out and looking down to see him waving his arms wildly. Our jumper still lay in a crumpled heap some distance away.

We immediately plunged down to get Baggett. As we descended he continued waving wildly and backed away from the helicopter. Upon touchdown, he ran up to the pilot's door, opened it immediately, backed off a distance, and continued flailing his arms. The co-pilot's head swung around. His wide eyes conveyed a sense of urgency as he mouthed silent shouts in my direction. I could hear nothing but I knew he needed me to do something. Then I realized he was yelling at me to open his door. Baggett and the pilot were already away from the bird when I swung around to see its entire port (left) side engulfed in flames. I had to get out of the bird to let the copilot out.

I grabbed my seatbelt latch and pulled on it. Nothing happened. I looked down and was horrified to see the repetitive loops I'd made in the seatbelt strap earlier. All these missions, the three feet of excess strap on the oversized seat belt had distracted and annoyed me. Now, around my skinny, twenty-four-year-old waist, I saw loops of seatbelt strap wound around the barely visible metal buckle I needed to pull to escape the burning bird.

In a panic, I yanked with all my might, but to no avail. That strap could easily hold twenty times the strength I had. It took less than a second for me to realize that if I did not compose myself and begin undoing the turns I had put in the seatbelt strap, I would burn to death. I would die in Vietnam.

One by one, I undid those turns of flat nylon strap as I sat in that burning helicopter. I thought I was beginning to feel heat from the flames. Looking up once I saw the co-pilot's head continue its crazy jerking turns as he sat wondering why I was taking so long. The closer I got to the end of the loops, the longer it took because the strap got longer as I undid it. The last loop was three feet long as I stretched my arm to clear it away from my waist ... there was the buckle. I grabbed it and yanked; the seatbelt fell apart and away from my waist in two sections.

I jumped out of the helicopter and ran forward, towards the co-pilot's door. Through the open doors across the cargo bay, dancing orange flames, fifteen feet high, blazed in the periphery of my left field of vision. I grabbed the handle of the co-pilot's door at the same time he'd decided he'd had enough of waiting for me. He pulled his emergency escape pins and the entire door fell off hitting me in the head. Luckily, I still had my commo helmet on. Somewhat dazed, I stood there as he exited the bird and brushed past me. Ahead of us Baggett and the pilot ran towards a wood-line fifty yards forward of the ship. The co-pilot ran after them and I followed him. As I ran, I summed up the situation. We'd been hit by some sort of high explosive projectile.

Somewhere in the hills around us, or worse yet, in the tree-line near us, he watched us and was preparing another shot. I imagined his sweaty tallow skin and dead black eyes and anticipated another explosion or a burst of automatic weapon fire to finish us off. As I ran, I looked west towards Laos. I felt an intense sensation, similar to goosebumps or prickly heat rash across the entire left side of my body. For some reason, that was the direction I expected to get hit from. I ran as fast as I could waiting to be shot or hit on my left side, the Laotian side. I almost felt the vivid images of hot metal fragments or bullets tearing through me. The skin on the left side of my body crawled as I ran.

Ahead of me, Baggett and the pilot slowed to a walk once they'd gotten to the tree-line bordering the clearing we'd run from. I could tell they were hesitant to enter the jungle. The co-pilot ran up to them. Eyes turned to me because I was last. I ran past them into the trees about five yards and assessed the jungle quickly. All my Ranger instincts kicked in. I looked for, and immediately found the spot we needed to be in. Nearby, but far enough away from our entry point into the jungle, I saw a large, thick clump of bushy vegetation we could hide in and still see out into our surroundings. This was perfect for concealment and even absorbing some shrapnel if we got hit again. "Follow me," I said. Without hesitation, they ran with me to the densest brush.

At some point, a truck raced madly by in the distance. I hadn't even noticed there was a road there. The driver must have seen the flames...

We sat and watched our helicopter burn. I listened for any sound. I looked at the pilots for any sign of a game plan, but there was none. We sat there forlorn and mesmerized by the burning ship. By now flames had engulfed both sides of the bird and my realization that I'd left both my machine gun and M16 rifle on board came too late. I believe one pilot had a .38 revolver and it was all the weaponry we had. To my thinking, we had nothing but a pop gun. I assumed Baggett, the crew chief, had been wounded but I wasn't sure. He sat there silently staring at the flames.

Bullets began "cooking off" as heat ignited them. They popped and hissed like a monstrous popcorn kettle inside the burning hulk our ship had become. Suddenly the pilot got up and announced that he'd forgotten his camera on the helicopter. He made a move to get up and go towards the helicopter which was engulfed in flame. Even without an enemy presence, there was no possibility of getting within reach of that helicopter. I grabbed him by the arm firmly and in a stern voice said, "Sir, you can't go back there." He simply looked at me and sat back down.

He was not thinking right. Suddenly, dismay and panic moved me. Till now, I'd been satisfied to find cover and concealment and lie there hiding from the enemy. What he said jarred me into a new sense of urgency and prompted me to action because I realized our situation was not going to solve itself. His words only made the situation seem more dire. I was the only one here with any jungle experience.

"You guys stay here." I got up and moved cautiously towards the clearing.

I'd been alone in the jungle many times before with F Co Ranger teams. That thought filled me with courage, hope, and motivation as I carefully surveyed our surroundings again and thought about our options. The black guy was probably still on the far end of the clearing. For all I knew he was dead. I stood up and gingerly walked to the edge of the wood-line. I positioned myself to have a clear view of the entire clearing and its immediate area. I could see the black kid on the other side. I stayed there a while to watch for movement, then I took a deep breath and walked out into the open space so I could scan the skies around it. My pulse raced; I was completely exposed. I peered into the sky in all directions. I did it slowly because I wanted to be thorough and didn't want to have to come back to expose myself again. I'd looked from left to right only a few seconds when, to my joy and wonderment, I saw the helicopter in the sky miles away. It was only a moving dot, far from our position. A surge of hope filled me. All of our lives, possibly our only hope of survival, hung on that lone helicopter so far away.

When I left F Co Rangers, I'd taken two souvenirs. One was a strobe light for marking positions at night in an emergency, the other was a directional signal mirror. I carried that signal mirror on all our flights and I had it in my top left pocket that day at Lang Vei. I quickly pulled it out and brought it up to my eye. I'd never used one before and quickly calculated that it was a simple matter of angle. The mirror had to be positioned so the sun would bounce off it towards my target. I peered through the sighting hole and feverishly adjusted the angle of the mirror so the light dot would appear and align with the helicopter. I had to steady my adrenalin-pumped hands on the mirror as I clamped it. There... I had the light dot. Now I had to delicately move it onto the helicopter through the sight. If I moved it too fast I'd lose that dot and have to start all over again. I gently adjusted the dot directly onto the helicopter in the distance. Then I moved it away, then back. I got the feel of it and started repeatedly flashing that helicopter. I kept this up and before long, it came. Relief washed over me.

A UH-1H helicopter, almost identical to ours, roared out from behind the treetops. The explosion of sudden sound came at me like some triumphant crescendo of horns in some victorious symphony. It was beautiful. Caution to the wind, I ran out into the clearing further and waved my arms madly. I was sure the pilot saw me.

He made one pass, circled back to where he came from, and disappeared. I ducked back into the jungle and ran to my guys. I squatted and elatedly told them the news. Soon, another helicopter roared in on us. It was a Cobra attack helicopter. He began circling the clearing nose down with all those beautiful rockets and machine guns (mini-gun). Joy welled up in me; I knew we would be saved. Suddenly, something inexplicable happened. To this day I don't understand it and I almost hesitate to write about it. The fog of war perhaps...

As I sat crouched with my guys, I felt a repeated, urgent tapping on my shoulder. Too much was going on so I tried to ignore it. Then I thought that one of the crew might be trying to tell me something. I turned and was astonished at what I saw. It was a reporter and his cameraman. I turned away from the distraction and tried to put it aside as I resumed watching the skies. The tapping on my shoulder resumed. Furious, I whirled.

"Do you know where the fuck you are? Leave me alone." I hissed.

"Please," he implored. "This story is worth so much money to me." I don't remember what I said but he sat down frightened and wide-eyed.

I heard it first, the unmistakable sound of a Light Observation Helicopter (LOH). It came drifting down and landed about forty yards away to our left, near a corner of the clearing. I heard it sit there, at a fast idle, for about fifteen seconds. No one came to us from the bird. Curiously, no one among our group moved. On a sudden impulse of sheer instinct, I got up and sprinted across the flat top towards the jumper who still lay motionless where he fell. I knew the LOH pilot would see me and not leave. As I ran, I once again felt that dread of vulnerability and total exposure. I ran what seemed to be three seconds but I covered eighty yards. I got to the guy and tried to rouse him. The most I could get out of him was a low, moaning sound. There was no recognition in his eyes. Reaching down, I grabbed his left arm and wrestled him up and onto my shoulder in the fireman's carry I was taught in Basic Training. It worked. He was lucky he was thin and I was strong. Even as I ran the sensation of reward came over me. The Fireman's Carry worked. I was saving him.

My strength surprised me and I ran as quickly as I could to the LOH with the weight of the man pressing down on me. When I got to the LOH, I opened the pilot's door and was immediately struck by the eagle insignia on the pilot's collar. The pilot was a Colonel. His rank made me hesitate and it struck me as odd that such a high-ranking officer would put himself in such danger. I threw my patient across his lap and turned to run.* I took two steps and wheeled back around towards the helicopter. I'd seen a case of phosphorus grenades in the bird so I grabbed one though I knew it would probably be useless. The damn things exploded further than an average man could throw them.

I ran back to my guys and heard the LOH taking off behind me. Several minutes passed and a "slick" helicopter just like ours came down to pick us up. As we took off I felt a great tension leave me: I felt able to breathe again. In what seemed a blink we were back in Quang Tri. One by one we were interviewed by a major regarding the incident. I tried to downplay both pilots' foolishness in making that landing, but the story could not be downplayed or changed. I'm sure heads rolled over the incident. I found out later that the guy I'd saved took a chunk of shrapnel right through his thigh in addition to his fall injuries.

After I left the major's office I took a slow walk and found a sandbag to sit on. It felt good to sit there alone in the encroaching darkness of the evening. Fate had allowed me to snatch redemption from the jaws of death. My newfound strength slowly drained from me as I watched the sunset. Soon it would rise, bringing a new day. I felt a chill.

I didn't know what happened to Baggett because I never saw him again. At first, I was told he had been wounded. That made sense because he had been so close to the explosion. Later, I found out he had been killed on Easter Sunday. He had volunteered to fly on his day off. He took a chaplain out to the field to perform a religious service for the troops and their bird got hit with an RPG upon landing. I got the news from a sergeant who knew me and was familiar with Baggett as well. I had just walked into the supply room to get something and was about to leave when I stopped because he was staring at me and his eyes seemed different. I still remember those bright blue eyes staring through me.

* I've been asked repeatedly why I put an injured man on the pilot's lap and not in the cargo bay. I don't remember any cargo bay. I write this the way I remember it ... and I don't know where the reporters came from.

"You know Baggett got killed, right?"

"What?" I was speechless. It was all I managed to get out and I simply stared at him. I walked around the company area in disbelief.

I never got to know Wayne Carlos Baggett. Though he was my assigned mentor and superior as crew chief of my helicopter, there was a certain abstractness and distance about him. I don't believe I ever saw him smile. He was just an average man with a very pink face and a blast of blonde hair—a short-haired beach boy look. I have often wondered where the name Carlos came from since he was a classic Caucasian.

We first met on the runway at Quang Tri as I stood eyeing the helicopter that I would be flying in for the first time as a crew member.

"Are you my new gunner?"

"Yeah."

"You know how to use a '60?" He glanced towards the machine gun.

"Uh-huh," I answered.

He backed up one step and pointed to the fuel port on the side of the helicopter. "You're responsible for fueling the bird. I'll show you how later."

"Okay."

"When the pilot says 'Coming up,' you make sure your side of the bird is clear and say 'Clear up right.' Same thing coming down. Check the ground and say 'Clear down right.' Got it?"

"Okay." I nodded nervously.

"Don't worry about it. I'll be saying the same things after you, but I say 'Clear down left,' understand?"

"Uh, yeah, I think so."

Baggett was the gunner on the other side of the helicopter as well as the crew chief. His voice was even flatter when he leaned into me and spoke again: "When we're coming up, out in the bush, usually the pilot will say 'Go hot.' At that point, you fire the machine gun. Fire till we're well away from the ground. Sometimes, though rarely, he might give you the order to go hot while we're coming in. You have to be careful here. You don't want to shoot any friendlies. Don't worry about it for now. I'll coach you over the intercom."

He said little else to me. He gave me a tie-down for the blades of the helicopter and showed me how to pull a blade to the rear of the bird to secure it. Though I'm sure he must have, I can't remember him ever speaking to me again. I flew on other birds and I flew with other guys. I'd see Baggett in passing. In just one month, I would fly two hundred and fifty hours and then, later, I flew with him that one last time when we got our helicopter blown up. Though I remember him waving his arms at me during the emergency, I don't remember him ever speaking that day. Even as we hid on the jungle floor watching our helicopter burn, I don't remember him speaking. It was as though he was never even really there. Baggett's death felt distant. My learning of it only saddened me temporarily. No tears fell and it was little more than a sad statistic at the time, an isolated fact about a man no longer there. Baggett seemed never there to begin with.

Years passed after my discharge before I made any military connections. My first tenuous forays into the past were hampered by memory and shards of emotion. I found out that Baggett's hometown was Tampa, only forty minutes away from me, so I began looking for his family. I never found a single relative despite doing a lot of detective work and making a lot of telephone calls.

Though I never really knew the guy that well, he lies gently on my memory: a small sadness from a distant time, a futile death in a noble but futile war...

He is a hero who died protecting a country that would not recognize him: almost as if he was never there to begin with.

31

Fifty Knot Smoke

"Coming up."

"Clear up right."

"Clear up left."

We lift off the Quang Tri runway a little after sunrise and head straight towards the Laotian border. I work the bolt of my machine gun back and forth. After I'm satisfied it is working smoothly, I slip the ammunition belt into it, slam it closed and settle back in my seat.

I have been in the Army for three and a half years. Two of those years have been in Vietnam. In two months, my time in the military and Vietnam will be over. I will go home. The war has dragged on for years and an apathetic public back in the United States doesn't care about it. Patriotism is dead and the phenomenon of the long-haired, peace-love-drug movement has evolved laterally with common sense and exists on an equal plane with it. I would always be puzzled by this paradox. The only people that care about this war are the enlisted personnel who joined to fight it, some officers, and a few of the Old Guard at home.

I will not die here.

We're cruising at several thousand feet. My Nomex flight suit flutters cool against my legs and chest. The afternoon sun has slipped to two o'clock high with a blinding glare so I reach up to my helmet and unscrew the knob that releases the tinted visor. I pull it down and now my head is completely enclosed. Staring out the door, I scan the horizon from one o'clock to three o'clock. Everything after three o'clock is of no interest to me because we have already flown past it. My eyes search and assess everything ahead of the bird, not behind it—ahead of me and not behind me. All I have to do is make it for two more months: sixty-two days. That day cannot come soon enough and I spend the majority of my time thinking about it. For over three and a half years I've struggled to control my destiny to avoid becoming a casualty of war. I escaped the meat grinder of conscripted infantry. I even stole glory by becoming a Ranger and then an aircrewman. My machinations to escape death have only brought me closer to it. I console myself with the knowledge that if I die, at least I will not die the unsung, anonymous death of a resentful draftee foot soldier.

"We're coming up on our next stop." The sudden voice in my head-phones startles me. I turn to my left and look at the back of the pilot's head.

Perhaps it's the heroin; perhaps it's the lack of it: I haven't been pay-ing attention lately. I've taken to stashing a couple of vials of the stuff in the quilted soundproofing that surrounds all the surfaces of the cabin. I simply unsnap a section of it above my head, stash my dope, and re-snap it. The dope makes the bad times feel better. It makes the good times feel wonderful.

The ground is coming up at us. It is dotted with men, fighting posi-tions and tents. I get on my machine gun though I know I will not be going hot because there will be friendlies in all directions when we land. My gaze stays on the ground below me as we continue our descent.

At a few hundred feet the pilot speaks again. "We're going to try this again because I want to see what the wind is doing. Gunner, drop a smoke grenade on the next pass."

The helicopter lurches forward. We stop our descent and circle for a new approach. I grab one of my smoke grenades and pull the pin after I know I have a firm grip on its handle. We bank three hundred and sixty degrees and start our run again.

We're coming in pretty fast. There is a soldier on the ground with his arms up guiding us in. He is some distance ahead of the bird. I reach out of the ship and drop the smoke grenade. Its primer pops loudly and I lean out quickly so I can watch it fall. My seat belt cuts into my waist as I strain to see it. I watch it arc through the air below me towards the man on the ground. It misses his head by several inches. I have to pay more attention.

We make our final approach on the third pass and I can see the widening ribbon of purple smoke, from the grenade, ahead of us as we come down again. "Clear down right," I tell the pilot though it is unnec-essary because we are landing on a flat expanse of brown dirt.

We touch down in a whirling swirl of dust and smoke. The purple plume of smoke from my grenade mixes with the wind from the blades of the helicopter to create purple dust devils that dance crazily around the ship. A figure in jungle fatigues runs through the smoke towards the helicopter in a semi-squatting position with one hand clamped to the top of his jungle hat. He approaches me with a searching look. I avoid eye contact because I almost killed the guy a minute ago. He leans into the bird and yells: "You guys have mail for us?" I stare at him because I don't really know.

The crew chief appears from behind me and stretches out an arm to him with a mail pouch; then he returns to his seat on the other side of the bird. The engine whines and we start lifting off again.

"Clear up right." I look around and grab my machine gun as we lift off. I'm still on my 60 watching the ground fade away below me when I hear the pilot's voice again.

"A couple of more stops and we might be going over the fence." He means Laos.

I feel the familiar knot in my stomach and my attitude turns pensive as I contemplate what the day might bring now. At about three thousand feet I take my hands off the machine gun after swinging it into the down position. I try to relax and force the familiar dreamy states that I enjoy cruising at a safe altitude. I feel safest near the clouds. This escapism to get away from reality only hastens it. Time moves faster when I do this but there is no slowing down the inevitable. There is only speeding it up. It's not that good to dream anyway. I need to pay attention.

A cool mist rouses me as we run through a cloud but the cooling sensation is over before I can revel in it. When we fly back out into the sunlight, the moisture is gone. I rub my palms against my thighs. The Nomex material is already drying and my eyes return to the moving scenery below me. In my helicopter, Vietnam is like a movie. One I must watch it till its end. It is a movie I can watch as a spectator most of the time till the real-life claw grip of fire, metal, smoke and sound draws me in as a player. It always happens suddenly and often unexpectedly.

We're descending. There is a large base coming up below us. I'm not sure where we are and it doesn't really make much difference. I'm always focused on my gun or what's in front of me. It may be another mail run but I'm not sure. If it is, I don't even know where all this mail is being stored in the bird. I never noticed; if I did I forgot. The crew chief is usually in charge of these details anyway. It's a good thing too because I couldn't care less. I just want to get out of here alive. My plan is to stay out of harm's way and kill anything that threatens me. My means to achieve that end are my machine gun and my wits.

"Clear down right."

"Clear down left."

The crew chief and I recite our short lines and we land. Our bird touches down with a light bump. Whatever this landing is about happens quickly on the crew chief's side of the bird. We take off again.

"Coming up."

"Clear up right."

"Clear up left."

32

Bodies in the Bird

Khe Sanh was the main staging area for operation Lam Son 719. We'd land there often during our trips in and out of Laos; sometimes we'd refuel there. Often when we brought soldiers out of Laos we'd drop them close by. On one occasion, our pilots had a high-level briefing with South Vietnamese Army officers there. I knew they were high-ranking because a guard with a rifle snapped to the port arms position and blocked me from entering that meeting when I needed to talk to the pilots. During Lam Son most of my flights were into Laos. I can only remember two or three occasions where we flew in support of that mission on our side of the border. On this day we were flying support for small units around the Khe Sanh plateau. Not much had been happening and I'd been getting complacent because of stress and my approaching ETS date. It was easy to do when we weren't shuttling soldiers in and out of combat. Khe Sanh and the area around it were still very dangerous because the North Vietnamese Army kept attacking it. Blocking positions and ambush sites had been put in place surrounding the entire plateau.

We were descending. The landscape below flowed in waves of small hills and valleys with larger hills behind them. Vivid green undulated in waves.

"Stay sharp guys. These guys got hit pretty hard last night." It was the pilot. The words pulled me out of my thoughts. I realized we were losing altitude.

I strained to see forward of the bird and after a few seconds, as we descended further, I could see them. I saw their pink faces first, then their hands waving at our helicopter. I grabbed my machine gun, stood up and looked towards them, alternately scanning the jungle as we approached, and then back at them. The pilot's approach was hard and aggressive. We banked suddenly and dropped quickly. We had barely

My gunner's view of the inside of a helicopter.

touched down when several of the men on the ground lifted and shoved the dead body of a U.S. soldier into the bird. Grim faces with hair flying in all directions from our rotor wash whirled around again to simultaneously lift and push another body into our bird. This time it was barely recognizable because it was wrapped in a poncho liner, perhaps several of them. We immediately lifted off but the guys on the ground kept looking at us. I could not help but feel that they wished they were on my bird.

We'd come up about ten feet when I was suddenly startled with the recognition of one of the faces down there looking up at me. There below me was one of the guys I'd known back at the Third Armored Cavalry at Fort Lewis. Even as I waved and yelled at him I realized there could be no reciprocal recognition. He would never hear me through the noise and he certainly couldn't see me. I ripped off my commo helmet and continued yelling and waving. He saw me but there was no recognition in his eyes, only the hundred-yard stare of a man who'd been in battle. We flew off.

Once we were at a safe altitude, I turned around to look at our sad cargo. The first guy they'd shoved in had no visible wounds. He lay there

184

on his side in a fetal position with heavy soot on his hands and face. I surmised he'd been in an explosion. Next to him lay the guy wrapped in poncho liners which were tied to contain the remains. There were no features to distinguish any body parts, only a giant round mass that shuddered and shook in flight. It was clear to me he'd been in an explosion as well. Bodily fluid leaked out of the improvised bail onto the cargo floor. We flew a straight line to deliver him to the second leg of his journey home. As we flew I turned around repeatedly to look at the bodies on my ship. My heart went out to them but it could not reach them. All my thoughts were simply reflected back to me. I could do nothing for them. I could only think of them and would continue to do so for a lifetime.

33

Shot Up

I'm plodding towards the flight line with my M60 machine gun on my shoulder. It is stable there because I hold it by the barrel. In my other arm, I cradle my flight helmet and somehow manage a grip on my M16 rifle. My flight helmet has been acting up. Communication keeps cutting in and out and sometimes it doesn't work at all. Must be a short or a loose connection. I make mental note to go to avionics to get it fixed.

Helicopters are coming to life on the runway at Quang Tri. I approach my bird where it is parked in its slot. The thump of blades and the whine of engines already starting up reverberates in the air and through my body. My shoulder is getting a little sore from the '60 that's been pressing into it and it's a relief to swing it off and mount it on its stand in my bird. My 16 goes into my gunner's compartment against the wall. I stand back and breathe in the morning air tinged with the perfume of aviation fuel fumes. Morning usually is a relaxed time because preparations for takeoff are a quiet affair. It is a time for reflecting on the day before and contemplating the day ahead. Today everyone seems busier than before. The rising sun dissipates the chill of northern South Vietnam and washes us with a welcome warmth as the thunder of waking engines stimulates the mind and body. Lifting my leg, I step up and over in a swinging motion onto my gunner's bench seat.

"How you doing?" It's the pilot or co-pilot; I don't know which. He doesn't know my name either.

"Good, sir." I never felt comfortable calling these guys by their first name. I always called them sir. Unlike most guys doing this job, I just was never in well enough to be buddies with any superior.

"We're going to Laos today, big flight, about eleven birds," he says matter-of-factly.

I figured we would be. I looked up at the pilot and fished around my thoughts for something to ask him. Nothing came to me so I looked back at my machine gun. As usual, I grabbed the bolt and pulled it back along the receiver, then quickly released it and listened carefully to the sound it made as it slammed closed. A tinge of guilt blurred my thoughts for a second because I hadn't cleaned it lately. It seemed to be working fine though. I lifted its cover and slid my fingers across the bare metal inside. My fingers came off slightly greasy and a little grey. I pressed the butterfly trigger and worked the bolt a few more times just to be sure, and I concluded it was clean enough. M60s are work-horses and they are very reliable. I thought about cleaning the gun later.

Despite being an experienced crew member by now, and despite the thrill I still felt from riding in these machines, the first flight of the day was a little worrisome for me. I rarely knew where we were going.

Most of the time, the rear of the bird lifted off before the front, giving it a bit of a carnival ride feel. Though I'd done this hundreds of times, that tilt and takeoff still thrilled me, even when flying into danger. I felt it as my gunner's bench pressed up against my butt. In a few seconds, we were airborne.

Multiple birds bobbed up and down as they attempted to fly a straight line and stay in a level formation. Once we got to about five hundred feet, I grabbed the ammo belt out of its box, fed it into the machine gun, and rammed a bullet into the chamber. I looked out to the front and back of the helicopter and saw other gunners in our flight loading their '60s also. I hung on to the gun and scanned the area below us till we were well into a safe altitude. Quang Tri faded away behind us and we were now on the peaceful leg of our journey. For the next twenty minutes, I sat serenely overlooking the world from my balcony in the sky. That time always passed too quickly.

"Here we go guys; we're crossing the fence, stay sharp." I sat up straighter and prepared myself for intense focus. Our helicopter formation crossed into Laos. I looked down and saw nothing but green jungle.

The border-line in the forest below me was of utmost importance but yet was invisible. I found this ironic. My life or death hung in the balance because of the boundary below me that nobody respected regardless of their nationality or army. The peacefulness of the flight faded and my heart raced a little faster. The thunder of our rotor blades pumped adrenaline into us as we charged through the skies of Laos.

The tension caused time to slow, yet, paradoxically, in no time at all we began our descent. The bird in front of us followed another bird which in turn followed yet another … and other birds followed us. We were going in.

My mindset going into an LZ is always the same. I challenge fate. I envision a yellow-faced son-of-a-bitch with an AK-47 hiding somewhere. It is more probable than not that somewhere within range of my gun someone is, in fact, watching. Militarily, it makes sense to me. We are perfect targets of opportunity. I grit my teeth and steel myself. I summon as much testosterone and anger as I possibly can. I become one with my machine gun. The butterfly trigger and the ends of my thumbs meld and send murderous intent through my arms and shoulders and into my heart. My eyes scan quickly. Show yourself and I'll do my best to kill you, you son-of-a-bitch.

Mottled green hues took on three-dimensional shapes as we descended. Those shapes bloomed into trees as the darker spaces between them became clearer. I crouched on my machine gun and waited for the pilot to tell me to go hot.

We flew so low now, I could see individual leaves on trees. The forest below us looked thin and I felt uneasy. We were too close to the ground for my liking. Flying in the open without cover in a helicopter this low was absolutely dangerous. It gave the enemy time to aim.

We are almost in the landing zone. I see it ahead of us.

What happens next confuses me. I hear a loud burping sound through the foam insulation in my helmet. Fairy dust sparkles and flashes of light twinkle in the air around me. I look towards the front of the bird and I see them there too. What in hell is going on? My instincts tell me we've taken fire and been hit. The pilot yells "Go hot" and I spin back to my gun and fire. The gun fires twice and stops. Two shots—like some scared child stuttering trying to say the simplest word. I cannot believe it. I drop the '60 and grab my M16. At the same time, I'm coming to the realization that my machine gun has jammed, it also dawns on me that I've heard nothing from the gunner on the other side of the bird, the crew chief. He's either been hit or his gun has jammed too. I point my M16 madly out the door and flip it on fully automatic. I hold my fire because I have only twenty precious bullets in its magazine. I know the landing is aborted because I feel the bird lurch beneath me as we desperately try to gain altitude.

I'm still holding my breath when I feel the tap on my shoulder. Surprised, I turn to see the shoulders and helmet of the other gunner. He stands hunched, silhouetted against the other helicopter doorway with the Laotian sky behind him. Behind his helmet microphone, his lips are curled into a grin. He points down. One Nomex gloved finger guides my eyes to the floor. It is stitched with bullet holes from one side of the helicopter to the other.

I looked up at him and we simply stared at each other, his ridiculous grin still plastered on his face. I swung back around because we were still pretty low. We were getting out of dead man's altitude quickly but after what had just happened, I started worrying about antiaircraft fire from heavier weapons. The NVA had those here in Laos. I watched the receding ground below us with distress and intensity. They could still knock us out of the sky with a .50 caliber machine gun or 37mm antiaircraft fire. We gained altitude as fast as possible but it wasn't fast enough for anyone on board, including the pilots.

"Everyone all right?" The pilot is swiveling his head around.

"I'm OK," I answer. Nothing else is said and we continue flying.

I marvel that this is all there is to it. The silence is almost laughable. We all almost died yet there's not much to talk about.

Our blades churn the sky towards home in Vietnam and I strain to hear strange sounds of malfunction from the bird. I hear none. I realize that everyone else is listening too. Any grinding, whining, or vibration could cause us to fall from the sky. We have auto-rotation capabilities; the pilots are trained for that emergency maneuver, but not from this altitude. I realize this is also the reason for the silence as we fly. Everyone simply wants to get home to Vietnam. It is like riding with a flat tire; the consequence of which is death if the wheel falls off. All of us know the danger and there is still a great distance to cover. We fly on. I don't remember how many birds headed back with us.

My eyes strain for some familiar structure, something: anything on our heading. I see nothing but I think the tension is easing. The pilots have it handled. We've made it this far and there doesn't seem to be anything wrong with the aircraft. Vietnam is not too far away. Relief washes over all of us. We are over a mile up and in some absurd inconsistency, Laos is beautiful despite its dangers.

It looks like we've made it. We land at Khe Sanh and get out of the helicopter. It is the kind of exit a person makes after a thousand-mile journey: slow, ponderous, deliberate. With a tug, I remove my flight helmet and put it on my seat. From the floor of the helicopter, my eyes follow an imaginary trajectory to its ceiling in the cabin but I cannot find where the bullets left the floor and entered it ... strange.... Then I think that the cloth-like material of the soundproofing might not show bullet strikes like the floor. It was then that I saw the bullet holes, level with my head, two feet to the left of the door. About that time, the rest of the crew came around to my side of the bird. The pilot grinned, his clipboard in his right hand.

"I've got a great war souvenir," he said.

"Let me see," said the crew chief as he and I both reached for it.

He got it first and we both examined the clipboard and its flashlight attachment. The flashlight had a bullet hole in it and the bullet was still embedded in it.

"There's another bullet hole six inches to the right of where this one hit by my ankle," said the pilot.

My helicopter had taken eight bullet hits. We stood there, in the sun with our flight helmets off, and laughed. After some silence and a few last looks at our bullet-riddled bird, I put my helmet back on and refueled our bird. The helicopter was not fit to fly to Quang Tri unescorted and we flew back that night, in formation, with some other birds.

We traced Route 9 from Khe Sanh to Quang Tri in darkness broken only occasionally by clouded starlight. A string of red lights in the sky was all we were to anybody above or below us. Route 9 wound below us like a meandering ribbon in the darkness. Though the road was used regularly, I was suddenly surprised to see a convoy of trucks below me in the night. They drove east in the same direction as we were flying. As I watched, the convoy came under fire. My thoughts whirled. Something had to be done here but what? Would we help then? I looked to my left towards the pilots but they simply flew on with the formation. Tracers streaked below me. I saw the flash of an explosion. Suddenly they were gone. After all, we were flying at over 100 knots. I thought about getting on the intercom to talk to the pilots. Then I thought again. They were probably already getting this information on another channel. I thought about the men down there in the darkness. Again I felt relief at not being an infantryman.

I slept hard that night with a newfound comfort inside the cocoon of my sleeping bag. In the morning I woke feeling unusually refreshed and very alive so I decided to walk down to the flight line to look at my bird again.

From a distance, I could see people gathered around my helicopter. When I arrived someone asked me if it was my bird. I simply grinned

Wreckage of a destroyed helicopter at Chu Lai.

and nodded. The two mechanics in attendance stared at the helicopter as if they were looking at a corpse: their faces serious and disbelieving. One of them took a thick stick chalk from his pocket and wrote in two-foot letters on the deck of the helicopter: DX: Direct exchange: Our bird would not to be repaired.

34

Redleg's Air

I don't remember what was so special about this South Vietnamese soldier that he warranted a ride on our helicopter all by himself, on a cross-border trip, from Laos to Vietnam no less. Strange how the madness of those descents into incredible danger blurred faster than the memories of the relatively peaceful flights back to base. That's probably why I don't remember picking up this nondescript, low-ranking man.

At ten thousand feet I turned away from my machine gun to take a look at him. I knew he felt my gaze but he did not make eye contact. He sat on the floor of the bird hunched over his M16, staring away into nothing. I felt a twinge of contempt for him. I was here trying to save his country from the invading North Vietnamese hordes and he had the balls to convey an attitude to me. Then again he didn't want to be here either, but he was in my helicopter, damned ARVN, he probably knew in his gut, just as I did, that the will of the South Vietnamese to save themselves, did not match the will of the North Vietnamese to conquer them.

We droned on. Sometimes, I'd time the beat of the blades into a rock song from back in the world. I'd zone out in my gunner's seat to Hendrix or Santana. I did so now.

Through the intercom, the pilot's voice abruptly tore me away from my music. "Just found out we're flying in Redleg's airspace," he said. At the same time, I heard the bird's engine wind down to slower RPMs.

The pilot had just been informed that we were flying directly in the path of artillery being fired ahead of us. These explosive projectiles traveled at the speed of a bullet and could weigh hundreds of pounds.

"We're going to drop quickly to get off this altitude so as not to get

Shot down Cobra helicopter salvaged.

blown out of the sky. We're gonna go down fast. Once we're close to the deck, blow away anything you see."

Before I could respond, I felt the roller coaster-like sensation in my stomach. My helicopter fell out of the sky as if the engine had suddenly died. I turned to try to communicate what was happening to our passenger. Even if he spoke English, he wouldn't have been able to hear me above the noises of flight. My arm made some lame motion that meant nothing to anybody but me. My attempt to assuage his terror only made it worse. His face contorted into a grimace. He looked exactly like a man in a helicopter about to crash was supposed to look: stricken with terror.

Turning back to the situation at hand, I felt the upward rush of air. This was actually pretty cool. Laos came up at us quickly. Just when I thought we'd crash into the jungle below us, the engine screamed. Blades strained. They sounded louder than I'd ever heard. The inertia of the sudden stop pushed me downward. I could feel the bird straining as we lurched forward no more than a couple of hundred feet off the ground. The pilot picked tree-top level at high speed for the altitude. I leaned out of the bird and swung my '60 in all directions. Crazed with adrenaline, I thought about just blasting away, then thought better of it.

It was then I noticed liquid streaming off the floor and out the open door near my left foot. It immediately turned into a mist as it went out the door in the 130 mile per hour flight wind. Puzzled, I traced the line

193

of liquid to the source. It was the crotch of the ARVN soldier we were transporting. He had peed in his pants. I thought it was funny, but I felt sorry for him. I moved both feet further to the right to avoid his pee, and we flew home to Vietnam that way: a laughing man on a machine gun, legs cocked crazily to the right, and a little Vietnamese man who had peed himself.

35

Zero One to Ball Game

I leaned on my "chicken plate" on the floor of the helicopter and peered into the bird as the mechanics worked on it. Today's flight seemed different. I'd been told to pick up this piece of flight body armor from our supply depot. I'd never seen one of these before. My fingers slid over cold porcelain-covered steel underneath a green cloth harness. These could have been cut out of old bathtubs, I thought.

Now, as I rested on its formidable weight, sober-looking mechanics were securing wooden crosses, wound with heavy, white nylon rope, to the floor of my bird.

Light washed our backs as the sun rose behind us. I looked towards the pilots to hear if they were saying anything about the mission. I had the feeling everyone knew more about what was going on than I did. This was usually the case with me anyway. I always felt I was valued more for my eyes and trigger finger than flight knowledge. Had a flight school degree been any standard for my flying status, I'd never have been accepted, to begin with. I usually hung out with wise asses and screwballs like myself. They were more fun, but here in Quang Tri, there was little light-heartedness. I kept my military demeanor to a minimum, but I kept my combat readiness and my detached attitude front and center. I had better control of my destiny this way. As an ex-infantryman and Ranger on my second combat tour, I stood on my own imaginary pedestal. I had to, lest I die in the cogs of the Army machine and its doomed endeavor.

I'd been told more than once I had an attitude while serving in the military. My feeling was that officers had the rank, but enlisted men did the work. Most officers and non-coms looked down their noses at me because of my non-compliant attitude, but warrant officers seemed more like regular guys. Easy-going and easy to talk to, they seemed more like my peers than my superiors. They depended on my firepower to keep them safe as much as I depended on them to fly me home.

The pilot looked at me. He stared before he spoke. "We're flying rescue today. If anyone goes down, we go in after them."

The usual misgivings of flying into Laos hit me harder than usual and we weren't even airborne yet. I looked back at the wooden spools of rope bolted to the floor of the bird. My immediate impression was that of some improvised rig the Coast Guard might use for rescuing a civilian at sea. I tried to visualize, but could not, a game plan that involved unwinding rope in some emergent shoot-down situation. Normally, I got to enjoy the morning's mist, fresh light, and mood at takeoff. I felt a tense pull across my stomach that usually didn't happen till we were approaching the Laotian border.

"What's this supposed to do?" I asked, pointing at the unweighted rope. "It'll flutter in the rotor wash and never make it to the ground. What about trees?"

He shrugged and climbed into the pilot's seat to do his preflight checklists. This always fascinated me. Though I sometimes (incorrectly) perceived pilots to be nothing more than aerial taxi drivers, they impressed me with their incredible bravery and knowledge. Few of these guys came from the hard streets as I did. Most were college brats who volunteered for the military. The Army took their education and honed it into a flying skill. Training and precise reflexes controlled these magnificent aircraft. Often, pilots flew straight into intense fire that destroyed aircraft and killed crews. I'd always marvel at their ability to fly a straight line into the jaws of the enemy while bullets peppered their bird. Flying back out meant taking more fire.

Preflight checklists fascinated me. Knowing nothing about them, they appeared to me to be a rhythm of textbook smarts: like tuning some thousand-stringed instrument. The pilots' fingertips twirled and his eyes flitted left, right, up, and down as he prepared for takeoff. He was joined by the co-pilot and the pace quickened as they both twirled knobs and tweaked dials. Soon our magnificent machine hummed and thundered the staccato that preceded takeoff.

Some of the longest expanses of uninterrupted forest in Vietnam lay along the flight paths to Laos. Other than Route 9, a dangerous artery that tracked from the South China Sea through the jungle to Laos, no other roads traversed this part of the country. This day our flight path took us over triple canopy forest that stretched as far as the eye could see. Whenever we flew over this much jungle, I couldn't help but wonder how many men lurked in that lush foliage below us. Once,

I threw an NVA canteen from 5000 feet just on the off chance that it might hit someone. I figured there was a one in a trillion chance that I'd cave in an enemy soldier's skull with the 150-mph metal bottle: a deadly wish spun on a roulette wheel from hell.

Somewhere past Khe Sanh, we landed at a staging area for South Vietnamese troops. While the pilots met and conferenced with South Vietnamese officers, I took the time to wander around a bit. I came upon American marines furiously packing supplies and parachutes to be dropped to beleaguered Vietnamese troops in Laos. As I watched, I slowly realized that their packing was too hectic and frenzied. I knew that the integrity of the parachutes was probably being compromised by the haphazard packing. Someone, somewhere, was in serious trouble. Watching this only added to my apprehension.

Soon, we were airborne once again and on our way to the Laotian border. As we flew, I realized we were steadily gaining altitude rather than leveling off. Higher and higher we flew, the earth below appearing different than I ever remembered seeing before from a helicopter. My mind conjured dark images of 37mm antiaircraft guns as we continued our ascent. We leveled off at ten thousand feet. I breathed in the unusually fresh, brisk air of this high altitude as it swirled around me in my compartment. My lungs heaved as I strained to suck it in under the weight of the chicken plate. We banked and began flying a large circle.

Somewhere during this time, I took my eyes off the horizon and peered down directly below the aircraft. What I saw astounded me. I'd never seen the high plateau we'd been flying towards because I faced sideways out of the helicopter. We were almost directly over a small mountain with its top neatly sliced off by forces of nature. It was a perfectly shaped, large plateau. I watched with horror and fascination as tiny puffs of smoke continuously peppered its entire top. I quickly calculated five to seven puffs per second as I realized each puff of smoke was an exploding rocket, mortar, or artillery shell. The friendly forces on that plateau and around it were enduring the fiercest attack I'd ever seen. Someone in the aircraft switched our communications channels and I began to hear transmissions about the battle unfolding below me. The plateau was being attacked by thousands of North Vietnamese Army troops. Mesmerized, I watched the intensity of the barrage increase. Many more little puffs were appearing than before. My heart reached out to those soldiers down there. I knew they were being decimated.

Resupply helicopters slid into view several thousand feet below us. Tracers (flaming bullets) came up at one ship and one round actually ricocheted off it as it hit. This surprised me since our helicopters had bodies made of corrugated aluminum soft enough to dent with one's fist. I estimated that these were .51 caliber machinegun rounds that had lost most of their energy. Rifle bullets certainly could not have made it that high.

I watched package after package pushed out of these helicopters fall trailing unopened parachutes. I felt sick as I watched them plunge to earth trailing that white, fluttering ribbon. Not a single parachute opened that day and the desperate men on the ground watched their desperately needed supplies crash to earth, off target, and probably get salvaged by the enemy. Meanwhile, we kept flying in circles.

Through all the chatter on my headset, I picked up on the fact that a major airstrike was on the way. My pilot confirmed B-52's were coming from Thailand. A strange countdown commenced over the radio.

"Thirty to ball-game."

"Twenty-eight to ball-game."

"Twenty-six to ball-game."

"Twenty-four to ball-game."

At "Zero One" to ballgame, Laos erupted. An unbroken flow of hundreds of huge, flashing explosions raked the landscape from right to left like invisible welders' torches. Over two miles up, I felt the reverberation through the air and through my seat in the helicopter. I leaned out of my ship, craning my neck and head upwards but I could see none of these enormous planes anywhere. They dropped their huge, deadly payload in one pass and the airstrike was over. I looked down at the plateau. The puffs of smoke had ceased. I visualized dead enemy troops by their mutilated rocket launchers and mortar tubes.

Within fifteen minutes, or less, the smoke from the airstrike clouded the air below us and drifted up towards our elevation. Soon we were enveloped in a brownish yellow, smoky haze that continued rising well past our altitude. We continued flying and I realized I was developing a severe headache. My breathing became labored as well. At this altitude, because of the thin air, my lungs struggled to get oxygen. In addition, I was inhaling thick smoke from the exploded TNT. After about 15 minutes, I felt as though I was going to pass out. I announced I was sick and yanked the communications jack on the end of my flight helmet cable out of its socket on the wall. I unbuckled my seatbelt and gingerly made my way to the deck of the helicopter where I lay down on the aluminum floor. No one else seemed affected by this combination of hypoxia and chemical sickness. These were the wages of cigarette smoking and dope.

The pilots looked back at me with concern as the other gunner left his seat and sat on the floor beside me to monitor my situation and look out both doors. I felt ashamed. I'd completely fallen apart and was totally useless on a specialized and dangerous mission. We flew that way all the way back to Vietnam. I felt better when we landed back near sea level and in clean air. Not a word was ever said about what happened. The others in my bird looked after me that day. They carried my dead weight through the skies of Laos, back to Vietnam.

Bomb Damage Assessment Reports indicated that entire companies of NVA troops were found dead in their positions. The forces that made these reports reported multiple columns of dead NVA troops. They never even got the chance to run.

I'd succumbed to altitude sickness but I'm sure stress factored into my condition as well. I was not the only one feeling the stress of the dangerous, daily flights into Laos. The extreme air missions left many of our people depleted. Too many hours in the air, too much air-to-ground combat; it all took its toll. Afterward, when we returned to our original base at Chu Lai, a hangover effect of malaise and tension cloaked the company. Enduring the massive operation left people a little overwhelmed. Business resumed as usual in the company area, but it moved in a jolting stilted limp. Idiosyncrasies became dysfunctions. Old grudges and animosities flared. Men got drunk and used drugs. I did too. Someone tried to kill the first sergeant with a Claymore mine. It was found under his hooch, directly under his bed, with the detonation wire leading away. We should have all had some downtime with a major investigation but there was a war going on.

36

Aftermath

For me, it all ended much faster than it began. Back at Chu Lai, after the big air assault into Laos, I developed a fever one day. With only a month or so to go till the expiration of my term of service (ETS), I got an even earlier out.

I went to the aid station, where they took my temperature, and immediately drove me by jeep to the 91st Evac hospital. There, a blood culture was taken due to my excessively high temperature and the doctor determined that I had either have a dangerous type of malaria or a staph blood infection. He had just lost a patient to a staph blood infection and I could tell he was affected by it. He wasn't going to risk it with me, so he put me on the first plane to a hospital in Okinawa. By the time I got admitted to the hospital there and more blood cultures got taken, the doctors could find nothing wrong with me. My temperature had returned to normal and three days later I was on a plane back to the United States. Seventeen sleepless hours later I landed at Oakland Army base exhausted. I had not slept in days.

I'd had enough. It should have been so simple. Sign a few papers, get some travel pay and get the hell out of there. Instead, the minute we walked off that tarmac at the airport, late in the afternoon, a lengthy processing nightmare ensued. It started with customs. Everything we owned underwent a thorough search. I even saw one guy's jar of Noxzema get probed with a thin metal rod. They were looking for drugs. Drugs had become a problem of epidemic proportions by 1970 in Vietnam.

Buses took us to the processing center where, first, we got fed a restaurant-grade steak meal. Then the standing in line to undergo out-processing began. We underwent physical exams, paperwork processing, uniform fitting, etc. I had not slept in two days. By the third hour, I could stand it no more so I simply stepped out of the line and wandered off to find a quiet corner to lie down and get some sleep. As I walked, a series of corridors, narrow halls, large rooms, and offices stretched out before me. I paid little attention to where I was going and then, unbelievably, I pushed open a door to an entire darkened dormitory full of bunk beds. Moving to the furthest bed in a far corner, my last thought before sleeping was a worry about getting in trouble or being woken too soon. A sleep of the dead fell upon me and it seemed only seconds passed when I was woken by a man with a flashlight. "Half this base has been looking for you. Are you okay?"

At first, I only nodded. Then, from his demeanor, I realized there would be no repercussions. I explained to this man, who seemed genuinely concerned, that I had honestly felt that I would drop of exhaustion. He seemed to understand. Three hours had passed and I felt refreshed. I hoped I would not have to wait in line anymore. The other guys were probably finished processing. When we arrived at the out-processing stations again everyone smiled at me. There was no anger, there was no problem. It took another hour for me to process out of the Army. I walked out of there wearing a Class A military uniform adorned with the few medals I was awarded for my Vietnam service, though I was now a civilian. Ahead of me, taxis waited in line for passengers. I opened the door to one, threw my duffel bag inside, and dropped onto the black vinyl of the back seat.

"How far to the nearest decent hotel?" I asked, looking at my watch.

"Not far at all. You just come back from Nam?" Dark querying eyes peered at me in the rearview mirror.

"Yes" I answered looking at the eyes, but he looked away and said nothing more leaving me feeling the conversation was unfinished.

At the hotel, I threw my clothes off, flopped onto the bed, and almost immediately fell into a deep sleep when a jet flew low over the hotel towards the nearby airport. The sound woke me in a panic. I flew out of the bed and hid under it before I realized where I was. Because of the loudness and intensity of the sound, my instincts had told me something would hit very close to me. My heart was still pounding when I fell asleep again because I was exhausted.

The next day, California sunlight bathed me and shined onto my new life as I exited that hotel. I decided to go to an old friend's house there in Los Angeles to visit before going home. I'd known him in the 3rd Armored Cavalry in Fort Lewis. Our reunion was heartfelt and he went out of his way to accommodate me, yet something was off. I felt out of place. I applied for a job at a California telephone company. During the interview, I was asked about my experience. Thinking of the most technical answer I could give, I told the interviewer that I'd been involved in aviation as a helicopter door gunner. He looked me straight in the eye and said that the telephone company didn't need door gunners. Though this was a portent of what lay before me, I didn't get it yet. The next day I got a job at a local grocery but I worked half a day and walked out. Everything I did in that store felt meaningless. In the coming days, I noticed that everything around me seemed somehow different though it was unchanged from before I went into the Army. I had trouble sleeping. I decided to fly home to New York City.

Back in New York, I didn't actually have to work. I had my mother's apartment for the time being. Languishing on the avenue with some of my old friends, I met many new young women who had only been juveniles before I left for the Army. Sexual conquests of these women and others I met seemed easier than they ever had been before. Men responded to me differently than they had before. I possessed a new tenacity and brashness, and people respected it though few cared about my Vietnam service. Many denigrated me for it. My new qualities gave me a self-confidence I did not feel, but rather saw the results of. I could no longer be bullied and in my first few years home, I prevailed physically in many run-ins with bullies from the old days. One particularly bad run-in with a violent bully resulted in my being arrested and charged with attempted murder. Invariably they would test the new Steve and usually regret it. Perhaps they felt they had to challenge the insolent cub who now possessed a stern gaze and non-compromising disposition. Sometimes, I would lose in these altercations because attitude did not always take the place of muscle. Within me, a wave of simmering anger grew day by day despite the fact that the vulnerable bullied child I was before I left for the Army felt more at home than the new me. Though I liked my newfound confidence, I did not like myself. Not much had changed at home, yet everything seemed different to me. It was I who had changed, and though that change was for the better, I was becoming a bitter alienated man, and uncomfortable in my skin.

At one point I enrolled in Queens College only to drop out two months later after being called a baby killer by an obese young woman dressed in the hippie garb of the day. Similar sentiments pervaded segments of society everywhere, and I navigated carefully to avoid them. Interactions with these people always brought on feelings of shame and doubts about my self-worth. During this entire time, I found myself spiraling deeper and deeper into substance abuse. In the early seventies, heroin could be found anywhere in New York, and I gravitated to it just as I had in Vietnam. By 1974 I had become a living example of the negative Vietnam veteran stereotype. I hit my low point in April of that year as I sat on my pullout sofa bed, emaciated from self-abuse and weeping as I watched the fall of Saigon on TV. The greatest endeavor of my life meant nothing. The United States had turned its back on the Vietnamese, the war, and the fifty-eight thousand soldiers who fought and died thinking their efforts were for a noble cause.

Listless, angry, and lost I'd wander the avenue in search of something to do or someone to meet, but people from four years ago had moved on. My alienation grew.

Around the corner from the avenue and two blocks down, a strip park stretched another two blocks along Queens Boulevard. I'd find some solace there being alone in the evening, on a bench by the flagpole. Sitting there morose among the trees in the dark and watching the cars go by brought a small amount of peace I rarely felt anymore. One night, as I sat there in my misery, I realized that the storage locker next to the flagpole probably contained the flag that was always folded up and put away at the end of the day. I stared at that locker for a long time before I got up and pried it open. Inside, beaming its colors at me, was the flag. I never said the words but I heard them loudly blaring in my skull. "This flag doesn't belong to you, you. It belongs to me." I took it and kept it for almost 30 years.

Several nights later, sitting there on the same bench, I saw the girl of my dreams sauntering down the sidewalk in front of me. Blonde and well-groomed, she was beautiful from a distance, even in the dark. In my best manner, and with elegance, I said just the right words to her ... like some lucky Hail Mary football pass. She slowed her walk, responded and we spoke for the rest of the evening. We had many things in common, including drugs. Weeks passed into months and at my insistence, a beautiful friendship turned romantic. She bore me a son and loved me but my heart was empty, cold, and cruel. I was not a fit partner for love, only passion. I would go on to mistreat this woman whom I loved in all the wrong ways and for all the wrong reasons. She'd eventually leave me, her only rational choice, and I'd spent a lifetime of remorse and guilt over my treatment of her. Eventually, when I built up the nerve to apologize, not asking for anything else, she would not hear of it.

We Had to Get Out of That Place

I was fifty-seven years old before I mellowed enough to be a good husband to anyone. I met my wife Linda and we've lived a very good, fulfilled life. I left the dissonance and tears behind me. Anger still remains, but I deal with it and reach out to Linda on occasion when the load gets too heavy. The alcohol and drug remedies of yesterday remain in yesterday because the temporary relief they offered was just that; temporary ... and the piper always had to be paid.

These days I fish, write, and enjoy the splendors of nature in the Florida sun. I think of the past, especially Vietnam, every day and I feel a grim wind blowing in the land I love and fought for. Every day I feel it is blowing a little harder than the day before, but I have fought my fight and earned my rest, though the aftermath never ends.

Epilogue

It has been over fifty years since Vietnam, and like most Vietnam veterans, I think of that war daily. The memories visit me whether I want them to or not. These thoughts are particularly strong when I think of the soldiers who fought and died in Iraq and Afghanistan.

Some time ago I made the decision to give back. Still troubled by past events, I thought I would do something for veterans. I joined an organization called Bugles Across America. The primary function of this organization is to provide live buglers to play Taps at military funerals, a longstanding tradition and VA benefit that has been long neglected. I played trombone in high school and figured the bugle would be easy. I was only partially correct. It turned out that a bugle or trumpet required much more self-control than other brass instruments.

With great trepidation, I played my first two funerals at Bushnell National Cemetery. The sergeant in charge there had reservations about my playing. He said, "You're so nervous I'm afraid you're going to fall out on me." Then the unexpected happened. I got an assignment to play Taps at the memorial service of Sgt. Keith Coe, killed in Iraq on April 27, 2010. This had to be a mistake. Somewhere between Ft. Stewart and me, the request for a live bugler forgot to specify that the bugler should be an accomplished player in a military uniform.

The sergeant at Bushnell National Cemetery, where I'd only played twice, offered to send a retired sergeant major with years of bugling experience in my place. My intellect screamed at me to do the sensible thing and take his offer. My ego would not budge and I could not let myself take the easy way out.

I could not sleep for two nights before the service. I played till my lips went numb. The morning of Saturday, May 15 came. It was time. My wife drove because I was not fit to.

We arrived at Oakridge Funeral Home in Winter Haven, Florida, to an array of fluttering banners, flags, throngs of press, Vietnam veterans, Army personnel, and grieving family. I could not think straight. This was as important as anything I'd ever done in Vietnam. We walked into the chapel, down the aisle to the front where Sgt. Coe's memorabilia were displayed. We both immediately broke into tears. During the service, I had to leave so I could compose myself. I went outside and talked to some Vietnam veterans. My heart rate at this point was out of control; I felt it thumping through my jacket and I knew I had to get its rate down to play decently.

A guy from the Vietnam Veterans Motorcycle Club looked at the F Co. Ranger patch on my blazer and asked, "Were you a Ranger in Vietnam?" I answered, "Yes." He pointed at a guy several feet away. I looked and realized that person he'd pointed to had the F Co. Ranger scroll on his leather colors. It was Ken, our own highly decorated, highly wounded Ken! The Ken that another F company guy I knew had saved during one of our company's most infamous firefights. I'd never been so glad to see anyone in my life. I bear-hugged him, held his face, and dragged him over to my wife. I suddenly felt more confident. I hugged him again. I told him to stand behind me when I played, protocol and policy be damned. "If anyone asks," I said, "I'll say you're with the F Co. Ranger Honor Contingent."

"Don't worry, if you hear movement behind you, it'll be me," Ken said.

The minutes ticked down. Everyone was in place. Ken stood under a tree fifteen feet behind me. Though standing at attention I kept swiveling my head slightly to say to him, "Keep talking to me." He did. He kept reassuring me. I bugled loudly, perhaps too loudly for funeral Taps but my performance was well into the realm of acceptability. Afterward, I walked to the government van, hid behind it, and wept. Relief washed over me and a flood of emotions poured out of me. Two minutes later when the ceremony was over, Ken walked up to me and asked, "Are you all right, man?"

"Yes, I am," I answered. "I'm fine, Ken. Just fine."

Glossary

AK47—Communist bloc rifle favored by the enemy in Vietnam

APC—Armored Personnel Carrier

Article 15—Non-Judicial military punishment for minor infractions

ARVN—Army of the Republic of Vietnam (usually used to designate one of its soldiers)

AWOL—Absent without leave (without permission)

Azimuth—Compass direction or heading

C4—Plastic explosive

Charlie—Slang for Viet Cong

CIB—Combat Infantry Badge

CO—Commanding Officer

Cong—Viet Cong

C Rations—Combat food of the era

Cyclo—A bicycle with a passenger bench on two wheels attached to the front

DX—Direct Exchange of an item due to damage, wear etc.

Eagle Flight—Infantry helicopter attack formation of ten or more helicopters

ETS—Expiration of Term of Service (discharge date)

Fatigues—The term of the era for army combat clothes

Fuse—A special cord that burns till it gets to the main charge to detonate it

Hooch—Constructed sleeping quarters

Intel—Intelligence

JP4—Aviation fuel

Mammasan—Common GI slang for older woman

Glossary

Mess hall—Army dining facility

MPC—Military Payment Certificates

Non-Commissioned officer—Any rank between Sergeant and Sergeant Major of the Army

Pappason—Common GI slang for older man

PX—Post Exchange: a store for military personnel

R&R—Rest and Recreation (or Rest and Recuperation)

Recon—To scout an area before committing troops

Reconnoiter—To scout an area before committing troops

RPG—Rocket Propelled Grenade (common enemy weapon)

VC—Viet Cong (communist guerrillas)

Index